HIS
REFLECTION

What God Longs to See in His People

Jeanne Metcalf
Copyright © 2016

First Printing,
International Copyright © 2016
Cëgullah Publishing
Copyright © 2022
www.cegullahpublishing.ca
Revised 2026
International Copyright © 2026
Cegullah Publishing & Apologetics Academy
All rights reserved

Textbook: ISBN # 978-1-926489-15-5
Workbook: ISBN# 978-1-926489-16-2

Cover photo ©istock.com
Cover design by Jeanne Metcalf.

COPYRIGHT MATTERS

This book is an original manuscript by the author, protected by international copyright laws of Canada. Therefore, none of this author's work may be reproduced, in part or in whole, or stored in a retrieval system, or transmitted in any form or by any means, electronic, mechanical, photocopied, recorded or otherwise for commercial use without the *prior written* permission of the author. However, it is possible to receive permission to use short quotations for personal use, or use in a study group study, or for permission to copy certain passages, or to make portions of the writings available for overhead viewing. Simply, contact the author[1] to request it.

---

[1] See Contact Page in Appendix

SCRIPTURE MATTERS

Many scholars challenge newer versions of scripture for their accuracy. Therefore, in the interests of being accurate, we chose to use the oldest version of scripture, the KJV. While there are many accuracy challenges within this version too, we find it much easier to validate original language words and thus authenticate accuracy. We have also noted that once a person becomes familiar with the KJV it becomes a little easier to understand. Therefore, all quotes in this book originate from the KJV, except the name of God appears as YHVH (yod, heh, vav, heh) or YeHoVaH. See Appendix for more information about the reason for this change.

DEDICATION

This book is dedicated to the Lamb of God, whose life upon the earth reflected the perfect character and nature of God and set forth the truest reflection of God for all people to see.

TABLE OF CONTENTS

Chapter	Title	Page
	Introduction	9

SECTION 1: CONSIDER YOUR WAYS

1	When Facing God's Reproof............	31
2	When Embracing God's Ways.........	43
3	When Encountering God's Authority	59
4	When Accepting God's Foundation..	77
5	When Recognizing God's Might......	97

SECTION 2: CONSIDER GOD'S WAYS

6	When Establishing His Plans............	117
7	When Releasing His Rewards..........	139
8	When Unveiling His Character.........	159
	When Dispensing His Purpose Intro..	176
9	When Dispensing His Purpose	179
10	When Revealing His Glory..............	197
	Conclusion.................................	221

APPENDIX

About King James Version.............................	232
About Jeanne Metcalf....................................	250
A Name to Honour..	226
Basics of the Ancient Hebrew Picture Language	239
Books by Jeanne Metcalf................................	247
Contact Information>...................................	252
Hebrew/Greek Word Index	
Blaspheme..	51
Dwelt...	213
Faith (regarding God's faithfulness).........	163
Glory...	203
Knowledge...	103
Mercy..	162
Profane..	52
Reformation (Root Word in Footnote)......	82
Shekinah..	202
Salvation's Message......................................	233
Scripture Index...	243
Sinner's Prayer & Lifetime Commitment......	237

INTRODUCTION

*I*N MY HOME, near my front door, positioned on the wall is a full length mirror. That mirror is there for a good reason. It is set up as a last-minute check point before leaving the house. I normally make a point of using that mirror before leaving the house because, on the one day that I forgot, I had a problem. On a certain, extremely busy day, when I hurried out of the house, running past the mirror without looking at it, I encountered two young children who innocently, and whole-heartedly laughed at me. Let me take you back to that morning.

It was a weekday morning when I was due to travel with my good friend and neighbour, to the U.S. As I stood in my bathroom mirror carefully applying my makeup, I knew that if I did not hurry, I'd be late.

Suddenly, the phone rang. Without thinking, I raced into the Kitchen, quickly picked up the phone and answered it. I ended the conversation as soon as I could, then hung up the phone receiver, grabbed my purse, and quickly ran out the door to find my friend, in her car, waiting for me in my driveway.

Quickly I entered the car, still gathering myself together after that last minute dash to the car. I asked my friend if we had just a few minutes so I could make a very quick stop at my bank's ATM, as it was on the way. As we arrived in the bank's parking lot, still in a hurried state of mind, I quickly exited the car and went into the bank. Right in front of the ATM machines were two little children in strollers. I smiled at them, and they smiled back at me and then suddenly they giggled. Cute, I thought. I completed my banking transactions, returned to my friend's car and got into the passenger's seat.

Earlier, at my home when I entered the car, I was busy straightening out things and my friend did not get a good look at me, but as I returned to the car she looked at me with a rather strange look on her face. Calmly she told me to look at myself in the car mirror. I pulled down the car visor, looked into the mirror and began to laugh at what I saw. You see, when the phone rang earlier that morning, just as I was finishing up my make up job, I was not quite done. That morning, I discovered I was out of blush so, as a substitute, I used lipstick. With a circular motion, I generously painted a large circle of red lipstick on each cheek on my face. In my hurried state, after answering the phone, I forgot to blend in the lipstick. Without knowing it, my face looked like that of a clown. All I needed to complete the face was a red nose. No wonder the children laughed!

From then on, before I go out to meet the public, no matter how hurried I might be, I try to remember to do a last-minute check in the full-length mirror, positioned at the door, just for that purpose. At that moment, that mirror becomes my friend, willing to tell all! Yes, its job is to clearly point out things in my appearance, good or bad. To me, it answers questions like, "Have I left behind any hair grooming tools such as clips or pins? Is my clothing in good shape and worn properly, *(you know, front to the front, back to the back and of course, right side out)*, and of course, is my blush properly applied?

Finally, I take a step back to see the reflection of my feet, just to ensure I am not wearing those old, comfortable scruffies I live in around the house. To go out, I must wear my better shoes, which are polished and presentable. When I leave the house, I gaze at my friend the mirror. It tells me exactly like it is!

All good mirrors, however, no matter where positioned, have limitations. Each mirror reflects only the surface or the outer appearance. It is, at best, a reflection of what is in front of it. That mirror cannot pierce into the inner person and reflect what lives there. Evidence of that inward being comes another way. We reflect it in our words and our deeds, through various situations that reveal our inner person, displaying to others what lies within. This aspect of ourselves, which takes opportunity for expression, is greatly affected by what we believe about ourselves, about others, and in Christianity, about God.

If we profess to Christianity, it is our expression of our faith that projects the image by which others see us, and the God we claim to know. If we demonstrate man[2]'s wisdom or God's wisdom, that is seen. If we project God's heartfelt love for others or surface shadows of our own love, that too is witnessed by others. On any specific day, if we face trying situations, it may bring out the best in us, but, on the other hand, it may bring out the worst, such as those moments when we are short with another, fed up with an incident, perhaps angry with one thing but somehow, we let the anger show up in a totally different situation. It is most unfortunate, but one

---

[2] When you read the word "man", either in scripture or this book, note that it refers to all humankind, not a specific gender.

moment's bad expression speaks far louder to others than a former long-term positive presentation.

THE BOTTOM LINE:
Momentarily, let's take a generalized overview of Christianity. As outsiders of the faith look upon Christianity, let's ask ourselves, what mighty they see. After all, they only see the outside appearance of Christianity, as believers express their living witness through daily circumstances. Eventually, however, after much exposure to Christians, eventually, observers see beyond the public image conveyed to them. Circumstances tend to reveal one's inner person of the heart with whom the world deals. This revelation, as seen by the world, is often not seen by the individual believer. Unfortunately, many believers are often the last to know about the message their "inner person" conveyed.

As believers, we know that the inner person of the heart is a major target of the Holy Spirit, and it is slated for a dynamic change. God's desire here is clear. It is, of course, to transform the inner person of the heart to align with the true message of Christianity, as God desires it be expressed. That message is better spoken to onlookers, including fellow believers, when the believer, experiences a deep, inner transformation of the heart such as the one the early followers of Yeshua's faith experienced. As we study that way of

Christianity, called "The Way" in early years immediately after Yeshua's ascension, the changes made in their life so much reflected Yeshua that onlookers made note that these had been with Yeshua when He was on earth.

> **Our Christianity, as we live it out, moment by moment, will either reflect Yeshua, or something different. The choice is ours.**

While this reflection is a work in progress, it is, of course, God's design for us to align with this all-important goal of correctly expressing Yeshua. Thus God, through the power of His Holy Spirit, invites us to allow a long-term, continual exposure of our inner person, to bring forth God's reflection, one we see as we look at Yeshua throughout the Word of God. Indeed, we can look at the Bible to further understand what God desires of us. According to James, the Apostle, the Word of God is for believers, a mirror:

James 1:23-25
"For if any be a hearer of the word, and not a doer, he is like unto a man beholding his natural face in a looking glass (mirror): For he sees himself, and goes his way, and straightway forgets what manner of man he was. But whoso looks into the perfect law of liberty, and continues therein, he being not a forgetful hearer, but a doer of the work, this man shall be blessed in his deed."

James, the author of this Epistle and half-brother to Yeshua, describes God's Word as a mirror to make a powerful point.

If one hears the Word of God but does not do it, that person is like someone who looks in the mirror but then goes away, forgetting what they saw. In other words, they simply go along their way without correcting anything about themselves.

In a natural mirror, perhaps their hair is wind blown, or their clothes are wrinkled but as they look in the mirror, they either don't see anything wrong with their appearance, or they simply just don't care. That person then, shows an example of the one who audibly hears what God has to say but the words fall on deaf ears. We might say, they are numbed, or blinded to what God says because of the way they perceive themselves.

On the other hand, if one hears the Word, they see the image of God within that Word. They see what they are supposed to look like. Realizing how far they fall short of that image, they obey the Word of God, not forgetting how God desires them to live. They pray and trust God that, through the power of the Holy Spirit, they can demonstrate to others what God is like. They hear the Word and do the Word, not forgetting how God wants them to live.

God's Word is a powerful mirror. It is like a true friend that tells us like it is. A person can then make choices to repent for what God shows them that is most unlike His character and Divine nature and then can seek God's help so that by the power of the Holy Spirit and the atoning work of Yeshua on the cross, they can become more like God. In that way, the reflection the people of the world see is none other than a work of God in progress.

Of course, that image is not perfectly expressed, immediately. No, that image requires a lifetime to perfect, but the believer, the personal representation of God, understands that fact. He or she does not wear an armour of pride that they have arrived, but rather a cloak of humility. He or she willingly asks forgiveness when offending another and makes restitution where necessary. He or she humbly serves others as Messiah's example taught. Yes, willingly, they follow God's command as they lay down their life for others. Their Christianity is not self-serving, but rather the exact opposite, selfless, serving God and fellow man. At least, that is how God designed it.

For sure, a serious believer in the Christian faith, exposed to the enlightening rays of the Holy Spirit, recognizes how far short they fall of the example of Messiah. Recognizing our humanity, these believers realize that, without God's continuous help, and our continual cooperation to yield to the Spirit's guidance, we simply won't be changed into the expressed image of His Son, Yeshua. To portray Yeshua daily in our behaviour, believers must mentally grasp the important fact that, first, we must die as the Bible describes:

Galatians 2:20
"I am crucified with Christ: nevertheless, I live; yet not I, but Christ lives in me: and the life which I now live in the flesh I live by the faith of the Son of God, who loved me, and gave himself for me."

Death to self, living that crucified life, is one obvious choice believers must make, but in doing so, it cannot be a one-time decision. It is a constant daily choice, as the Apostle Paul declared in his first letter to believers at Corinth, "I die daily"[3]. Most Christian believers, followers of the Way, often go about their daily business and consciously forget that aspect of the faith that we see in the mirror of the Word.

Indeed, every believer needs God's help to stay in the daily, moment by moment, expression of a life dedicated to God's service, including the command of God to love God above all things and our neighbour as

---

[3] 1 Corinthians 15:31 I protest by your rejoicing which I have in Christ Jesus our Lord, I die daily.

ourselves[4]. That is a large commitment, far greater than any human being readily assumes.

Unfortunately, looking with a generalized view of Christianity [5], one more time, we see that many believers, for numerous reasons, buy into only the surface elements of Christianity. Those elements are exterior signs of Christianity, that which expresses a faith in only an outward appearance.

For example, a certain believer meets weekly with Christian believers, however, during the week at home, at work or at other places, Christianity's lifestyle, as God desires, is not carried out. These believers regularly expose or even enjoin themselves to things this world presents to them as good or even profitable but these same things the Bible clearly states are harmful. Rather than deny themselves the pleasure and enjoyment of those worldly things, or a possible rejection by their peers, they convince themselves it is alright to take part in such things. Many make excuses

---

[4] *Deuteronomy 6:5   And you shall love YeHoVaH your God with all your heart, and with all your soul, and with all your might. Luke 10:27 And he answering said, You shall love the Lord your God with all your heart, and with all your soul, and with all your strength, and with all your mind; and your neighbour as yourself.*

[5] A generalized view incorporates every denomination of Christianity, everywhere. This term means the author does not single out one particular group of believers, worldwide. It means, as it say, a generalized overview.

that God understands, or it is antiquated to believe such, and such is wrong.

Then, on Sunday, or whatever day they meet for worship, they go to church, wearing what many call a plastic face, effectively wiping their mind and conscience clean from all ungodly weekly activities. Wearing a party face, they enter church fellowship. They sing; they clap their hands; they listen to the Word as it is brought forth from the pulpit; they smile at everyone and later leave that service assured, by their church attendance, that they have done their Christian duty.

What about the other 6 days of the week prior to their day of worship? What about the reality God saw in their hearts and they, unfortunately, failed to notice? What about the next 6 days about to transpire? These things, once again, fall into the category of looking into the mirror of the Word of God and walking away, completely forgetting about the reflection God intended them to mirror to the world.

Serious believers, those who wish to love God with all their being, know that kind of Christianity offends both God and man. To be frank, the Bible addresses this behaviour:

Introduction

2 Timothy 3:1-7
"This know also, that in the last days perilous times shall come. For men shall be lovers of their own selves, covetous, boasters, proud, blasphemers, disobedient to parents, unthankful, unholy, Without natural affection, trucebreakers, false accusers, without self-control[6], fierce, despisers of those that are good, Traitors, heady, highminded, lovers of pleasures more than lovers of God; **Having a form of godliness, but denying the power thereof:** *from such turn away[7]. For of this sort are they which creep into houses, and lead captive silly women laden with sins, led away with various lusts, ever learning, and never able to come to the knowledge of the truth".*

There it is, in the mirror of the Word, "having a form of godliness, but denying the power thereof". This is not Christianity's best foot forward by any means! Christianity of the Bible is very different. God's form of Christianity is commitment, and not just an outward commitment, but an inward commitment that requires one hundred percent of the believer! Most people in our world today don't understand the deeper meaning of that word "commitment" today, let alone a one hundred percent obligation to serve God with their entire being. Nevertheless, that is what God demands of those who call themselves by His Name.

---

[6] KJV says incontinent.
[7] Bold and italics the author's addition.

THIS STUDY'S DESIRED RESULT:
If you keep in mind these thoughts, written earlier in this chapter, you have the target of this Bible Study. It is a course designed to expose the "heart" behind a believer's Christianity, and thus, their expression of Yeshua. Its intent is to hold the "mirror of the Word" right in front of every person taking this course, including the teacher.[8] Its desired result is to eliminate what God, Himself declares offensive, as stated in His Word. It is also to ensure that believers enjoy a true, fulfilling faith in their relationship with God, and do not simply give the Lord "lip service", resulting in a vain or empty religion.

Matthew 15:8-9
"This people draws near unto me with their mouth and honours me with [their] lips; but their heart is far from me. But in vain they do worship me, teaching [for] doctrines the commandments of men."

---

[8] By teacher, I also mean me as I write this course and, later on, teach this course.

Relationship with God, as He designed faith's goal, is the theme we'll explore in this Bible Study. It is, therefore, designed for the serious Bible student, the one who wishes to really know their God, and then, through their life, wherever that road may take them, reflect a proper image of God to others. This Bible Study, (textbook and accompanying workbook) is designed for those who truly wish to make Yeshua Lord and Master over every aspect of their lives.

My dear reader, this Bible Study is, therefore, neither for the timid, nor for the casual Christian. It's intended for the serious believer who honestly, and perhaps even desperately, desires to take a good hard look into the mirror of God's Word for the sole purpose of obeying it. If this is your attitude, dear reader, determine to walk away from this study, carrying with you, each moment of every day, a definite response to what you've learned about God's Word. This means you will not set aside what you gleaned in His Word but rather, you will hold, intact, the memory of what you saw of your God, in the mirror of His Word ... *and having noted* how far short you fall of that image, determine, with God's help, to yield to the leading of the Holy Spirit, to produce life changes for the greater glory and honour of God.

So, dear one, if you are a believer who is truly serious about your Christianity and you desire to open wide a door to the Holy Spirit, to examine your life closely, intently, and thoroughly, you are ready for this course. I invite you, therefore, to pray the prayer on the next page, or pray one of your own with similar content. Then, take out the workbook and before God, make a serious commitment to allow the Holy Spirit to do a work in you, one in which you ask Him to help you to follow His lead and determine to not resist Him in any way.

Determine, with His help, beloved, to get through this course even if it seems that your life is turned upside down and inside out and you feel it cut deep into the heart. If that happens, remind yourself that the Word of God is designed for just that purpose. Its aim is to intentionally allow the Holy Spirit to cut to the heart, to expose what lays deep inside so "you" can identify what lies therein, and with God's help, learn to deal with it. God, of course, already knows what's there. It is we, His children, that often overlook what's so obvious to God. Unfortunately, we are often the last ones to know!

Also, in this introduction, in overviewing Christianity in general, references were made to believers with comments such as "they", or "them" or other pronouns referring to another. Generalizing Christianity, as done in this chapter, served the purpose of outlining an overall problem, however, that approach will never work when exploring a resolve for that problem.

Therefore, as we move into this study, that generalized viewpoint changes, no longer to how another behaves, but rather to look at things in the first person, asking the question, how do "I" behave. After all, that is the only way any Bible Study works, right? So, be brave dear one and join with many other committed believers, including this author, who desire the Lord to perform a Holy Spirit driven "face lift" so the image, which God sees first, and the world sees second, reflects the face of Yeshua as God intended.

Before closing this introduction, before you pray the prayer on the next page, please understand that God takes your Christianity very seriously. He will answer that prayer! As He does, keep in mind, there is an entity, an adversary, who has no desire for you to look like Yeshua. The more unlike Yeshua a believer lives in this world, the less effective is that believer and their witness, and thus, the happier is the adversary. Know therefore, if ha satan can prevent you in any way, in pursuing God, as you seek to become more like Yeshua, he will do it; and he will also readily use whatever tools he can to discourage you to walk away from your determined course of action.

Whenever any believer determines to produces good fruit for God's Kingdom, if they are pushing ahead and/or pushing back adversarial lines, they will encounter resistance. The first course of action is not to run! It is to resist the adversary, dear one! Therefore, in taking this course, ask the Lord to help you recognize the tactics of the adversary. Ensure you wear your spiritual armour and resist the urge to quit or to shrink back. Determine, with God's help, you'll make it to the other side. After all, doing that is following the lead of your Lord and Master, Who, for the joy set before Him, endured the cross!

A PRAYER
BEFORE DOING THIS BIBLE STUDY

Heavenly Father:

This day I come to You, the God of Abraham, Isaac, and Jacob, Who gave us Yeshua. In His Name, and through the shed blood of the Lamb of God, I humbly bow before You, expressing my desire to live my life before Your Face as you command, as one who loves You with all my heart, mind, soul, and strength. It is my prayer that I reflect Your character, just as did Yeshua. May my relationship with You be revelatory of what hides deep within, even in the hidden recesses of my being. May my contact with my fellow man flow out of my relationship with You, exposing Your heart as I learn to function, in one mind and heart, with my Lord and my God.

Please open my eyes that I might see what behaviours operate in my life that, first, offend You, and second, that present an improper image of Your Son, Yeshua and the heart of true Christianity. Please help me to push through any roadblocks or interference that stands between me and the fulfilment of this prayer.

Help me to sort through the many facets of my religious belief system, including all that I hold dear, so that my faith will be thoroughly founded on the Word of God, and from that foundation flow only the true teachings of God.

Help me to release anything, including wrong doctrines, teachings, practices, behaviours, or attitudes that I possess and yield to, *which are **contrary** to the Word of God*. Please show me, loud and clear, any ways in which I, in error, honour You with only lip service. Help me to embrace the heart-felt experience of true Christianity that You so desire for me.

Lord, according to the Word of God in Hebrews 7:25,[9] Yeshua saves to the uttermost, all those that come to God by Him, since He ever lives to make intercession for them. I draw near, therefore, to my Yeshua, in the process of being saved to the uttermost. I express my gratitude that He ever lives to make intercession, whatever is necessary, for me to obtain the ends of the faith, held in the heart of God, for my life as a Christian believer.

Impart Your perseverance into my spirit to enable me to be shaped into Your form of Christianity, implanting both the desire and ability, to endure to the end of my days here on the earth!

Thank You Lord for answering me. AMEN

***

---

[9] *Hebrews 7:25 Wherefore he is able also to save them to the uttermost that come unto God by him, seeing he ever lives to make intercession for them.*

Now, having prayed this prayer, know the answer is on its way. From this moment on, and long past the time this course ends, God will present opportunities for you to experience, things such as those to help you refine your faith life, making you look, more and more, like Yeshua.

Whatever you do, don't become discouraged, dear one, and please don't quit! In the circle in which you live, you may be a forerunner, and one God can use, as He did the believers, in the early, first century church: *"to turn the world upside down!"*[10]

Beloved, press on and press into God! On the day you stand before Him, you'll be glad you did!

---

[10] *Acts 17:6 And when they found them not, they drew Jason and certain brethren unto the rulers of the city, crying, These that have turned the world upside down have come here also.*

SECTION 1

Consider Your Ways

"Now therefore thus says YeHoVaH Tseva'ot
Consider Your Ways"
Haggai 1:5

WHEN FACING GOD'S REPROOF

1

"I will stand upon my watch, and set me upon the tower, and will watch to see what he will say unto me, and what I shall answer when I am reproved."

Habakkuk 2:1

PRIOR TO THE destruction of Solomon's temple at Jerusalem by King Nebuchadnezzar, Habakkuk, a prophet called by God, began to speak the Word of YeHoVaH to God's people living in Judah at that time. In the opening chapter of the book of Habakkuk, we hear how the prophet assessed the evil around him, seeing it prospers greatly, and wondered why it was so. Habakkuk had many questions about this evil that he saw flourishing.

Let's hear it from Habakkuk's lips:

Habakkuk 1:1-4
"The burden which Habakkuk the prophet did see. YeHoVaH, how long shall I cry, and you will not hear! [even] cry out unto you [of] violence, and you will not save! Why do you show me iniquity, and cause [me] to behold grievance? for spoiling and violence [are] before me: and there are [that] raise up strife and contention. Therefore, the law is slacked, and judgment never goes forth: for the wicked does compass about the righteous; therefore wrong judgment proceeds."

Habakkuk asked, in modern English: "Why does the righteous person suffer, while evil continues to succeed? Wickedness surrounds Your People and wrong judgments occur. Why does Your Judgment not come forth, YeHoVaH? Why, YeHoVaH? Why?"

Habakkuk believed in God's sovereignty, which ruled in all circumstances and in all things, and not just in Israel, but in all nations, yet these current events in Judah, as Habakkuk observed them, troubled him. Why doesn't God act? How can unrighteousness rule in such a manner? Those events that Habakkuk observed, simply did not line up with his understanding of God.

From his words in chapter 2, "I will watch to see what he will say unto me, and what I shall answer when I am reproved"[11], we understand that Habakkuk left room in his thinking for misunderstanding how God works. These words show us that Habakkuk was open to God for correction. He wanted God to enlighten him so he could understand the situation. Chapter 2 continues to relate God's conversation with Habakkuk. in response to his question.

Habakkuk 2:4-7
"Behold, his[12] soul which is lifted up is not upright in him: but the just shall live by his faith. Yes also, because he transgresses by wine, he is a proud man, neither keeps at home, who enlarges his desire as hell, and is as death, and cannot be satisfied, but gathers unto him all nations, and heaps unto him all people: Shall not all these take up a parable against him, and a taunting proverb against him, and say, Woe to him that increases that which is not his! how long? and to him that ladens himself with thick clay! Shall they not rise up suddenly that shall bite you and awake that shall vex you, and you shall be for spoil unto them?"

---

[11] *Habakkuk 2:1*
[12] When KJV spoke of humanity as a whole, they said, "man". When you read that word, or hear another person speak in reference to the scriptures and the term, "man", know it refers to all humankind, not a specific gender.

God speaks to Habakkuk regarding the situation that disturbed him so. In more modern English[13] YeHoVaH said:

Men rise up and appear successful to onlookers, but God sees what is in their soul. Look deeper Habakkuk! Look at what is inside, for one who is just, in God's eyes, is one who lives by faith. The proud heart sins with wine (as he drinks too much of it) and so he doesn't tend to his own household, his own family, his own blessings that God gave to him. His house is not in order.

Such a person's desire is insatiable. Like hell and like death, it's never satisfied. In other words, he is never content with his lot or things in his life. He has no peace, no place of rest. His soul is restless. *(Such a soul will wander aimlessly looking for satisfaction, but it will not find it!)*

This one who gathers all nations and brings forth all manner of people to himself, for his own gain and self-satisfaction, will find it will not satisfy him. Those that he drew to himself will eventually take up a cause against him. They will not speak well of him. They see

---

[13] This is an expanded version of the meaning of the scripture, written by the author to help readers grasp its meaning a little easier. If you are unsure of the comments, check a commentary to understand further.

that he was increased with goods, became wealthy, living comfortably, with things that were not his own.

In the end, all these things turn to bite that very man, yes, one morning, these things no longer stand afar off, but they awake and suddenly, without warning, this man becomes their spoil, their booty. He becomes their prey.

This is much like the Psalmist discovered as we read Psalm 73[14]. He too saw evil prospering but then, he obtains God's point of view:

Psalm 73:16-20
"When I thought to know this, it was too painful for me; Until I went into the sanctuary of God; then understood I their end. Surely, you did set them in slippery places: you cast them down into destruction. How are they brought into desolation, as in a moment! they are utterly consumed with terrors. As a dream when one awakes; so, O Lord, when you awake, you shall despise their image."

Once the Psalmist perceived their end, he understood. Habakkuk, through God's conversation with him, soon discovered the end of those who planned wickedness in his day.

---

[14] In your homework, you will study more of Psalm 73 so you can obtain more background information.

Besides the immediate lesson we learn from both Habakkuk and the Psalmist, there is another good lesson to observe here. As we look at both the prophet and the Psalmist, we recognize them as earnest believers of the faith, with great love for God and God's people, yet, their knowledge of God, as they faced the situation, was not adequate for that situation. Both Habakkuk and the Psalmist learned to look to God to show them what was really going on. Habakkuk bravely waited for his correction, and as one reads Psalm 78, we can see the Psalmist felt that he was foolish, even ignorant of the ways of God:

Psalm 73:20-26
"As a dream when one awakes; so, O Lord, when you awake, you shall despise their image. Thus my heart was grieved, and I was pricked in my reins. So foolish was I, and ignorant: I was as a beast before you. Nevertheless, I am continually with you: you have held me by my right hand. You shalt guide me with your counsel and afterward receive me to glory. Whom have I in heaven but you? and there is none upon earth that I desire beside you. My flesh and my heart fail but God is the strength of my heart, and my portion for ever."

Both the prophet Habakkuk, and the Psalmist took their problem to YeHoVaH, and each one opened himself up before God for the purpose of learning. They both knew that no matter how much they already knew about YeHoVaH, they needed to remain teachable.

REMAINING TEACHABLE

What we gain from Habakkuk and the Psalmist regarding learning, we can carry forth into our own environment, the world in which we live. Often, as we live out our faith before God in that world, things arise which we do not understand. Sometimes, trying as hard as we can to reconcile things to our faith system, it just doesn't line up with what we've learned about God. From those circumstances, there may arise a finger negatively pointing at God. At that moment in time, we have several choices. How should we respond?

Let's look at two probable responses to the problem of situations, where the initial or surface evidence points to an ungodly conclusion, namely, showing God as *prejudice, biased or unfair*.

> **Solution # 1:** to react with disappointment, hold resentment towards God. The sum of these things results in anger towards God; they turn their backs on serving Him, shut the door and walk away.

To respond with Solution # 1, (which, by the way, really does happen), the issue is not resolved. Eventually, that choice results in bitterness, unforgiveness and more things besides, all piling up to form a resistant barrier, at first to God, and later, towards others. This is certainly not a good solution, as it does not resolve the problem, but simply compounds it.

As this one, who earlier aligned with the faith, now makes friends with anger, disappointment, and bitterness, without knowing it, they imprison themselves. From that prison house, they set up high walls of doubt and disbelief, often with bars of hopelessness.

As time goes by, unless the person willingly opens their minds to learn truth and move past the stumbling block they fell upon, they will literally close the door towards any further knowledge of God. If they continue to hold on to their bitter viewpoint about God, once more without knowing it, they inadvertently form erroneous doctrine and if they turn their backs and walk away, in effect they adhered to a false spirit, the one who led them to become embittered against God. One who continues to embrace these things, normally, makes no room for any possibility of correction.

How much these dear ones need the faithful prayers of those who know them. It is horrible to think that these souls are deceived into thinking that their knowledge about God, no matter how deep, is all that there is. Often, these disappointed and frustrated people prefer to hold on to their erroneous teachings than venture on a pathway to reject them. Some conclude Christianity, God and all associated with it, is worthless and empty, a non-reality. Sadly, they tossed out the baby with the bathwater!

God's heart breaks for those individuals who slammed the door in that manner. Often, they also close it to all who taught them, as well as all with whom they formerly associated. How desperately they need prayer! Unless they release their anger, bitterness, and whatever else rages within them, it is only downhill from there! Not a good scenario.[15]

> **Solution # 2:** respond like Habakkuk who came before God to wait for God "to see what he will say unto me, and what I shall answer when I am reproved." This solution uses an open mind and asks God to correct him wherever he is in error.

In this approach, one asks God for correction, for help in aligning more correctly. He or she uses the situation for a far better purpose: to draw closer to God. This, of course, is the better solution.

---

[15] If you know someone like this, please take some time and pray for them. God dearly loves them and desires their return to His loving, restoring Arms.

To respond with Solution # 2, one concludes that, no matter what knowledge they have of the Word of God, they do not know everything that there is to know about God. This approach shows a willingness to examine their own, current faith system, to see if it is out of line with the true realities of God, and then correct the problem. This solution does not accuse the Bible, the Word of God, as the problem. *It rather says* that one's own understanding of the Word of God, of what they have been taught on that subject, or theory, may not align 100% alignment with truth. They are open to learn the truth, so they come into alignment with what the Word of God ***really teaches***.

As we look at Habakkuk's example, we can see his willingness to learn in an area where he perceived things incorrectly. Habakkuk faced God, bringing to Him, with great respect, what troubled him. He believed that God would show him where his thinking went wrong. He was opened to hear God's rebuke. That is always a better solution. No believer, no matter how much biblical training or schooling, can ever say that they know it all.

More than one preacher, in pursuing their degree, has come away from their time of learning with certain knowledge or compilations of biblical data, yet through it all, did not learn to develop a deeper relationship with God. Unfortunately, many times, the degree has been about the educational standard alone, and not about the relationship to which they are called. It is imperative that as we learn Biblical information about YeHoVaH, we see it as an open door to help us in our relationship as we get to know God. It is important that we know God, not just about Him!

CHAPTER'S SUMMARY
Our opening verse spoke of Habakkuk who stood before YeHoVaH, waiting for God's corrective word. While Habakkuk held many biblical teachings to help him grasp the concepts of the God of Abraham, Isaac and Jacob, the evidence seen in his day seemed to point a finger at God, declaring God to be unfair. Knowing God to be irreproachable, Habakkuk realized he must be missing something in his understanding of God.

God responded to Habakkuk's inquiry, not to clear His Name, but to help Habakkuk understand the bigger picture. From Habakkuk's problem to its solution, he demonstrates the importance of remaining teachable, willing to accept God's reproof. Accepting God's reproof to correct our ways, as well as understand God's Ways, is something every Christian believer should keep in mind:

Knowing about God & knowing God personally are two different things.

WHEN EMBRACING GOD'S WAYS

2

"He made known his ways unto Moses, his acts unto the children of Israel."

Psalm 103:7

*R**EADING THE FIRST* five books of the Bible, we see the initial beginnings of our universe and of mankind upon the earth. Also, we find recorded the earliest beginnings of the nation through which God chose to reveal Himself to the world: *the nation of Israel.* Through this nation, called by God to live separated unto Him alone, God chose to reveal His Divine Nature, as well as His mighty power. This people, whom God called chosen, were a peculiar treasure in God's eyes and received a unique opportunity, far greater than any other nation upon the face of the earth, for they were chosen to know God!

What did they do with that opportunity? Did they take the best advantage of their invitation to know the creator? As we read through the Pentateuch[16], looking specifically at those whose life God intercepted with the privilege of learning about Him, we see that only some took up the opportunity to really know God, but most did not. As our opening verse in this chapter from the book of Psalms declares, Moses, (God's chosen leader), knew God's ways, but the children of Israel knew His acts.

In this one verse, the Psalmist lays out before God, two possible relationships. One relationship shows a deep, effective relationship with God, in the way Moses knew God. (Moses knew God's ways.) That relationship was fruitful for both God and Moses, and it endured the test of time. The other relationship was the way the bulk of God's people responded to God. That relationship resisted the true knowledge of God as it did not penetrate the barriers of a self-serving people. That type of relationship was not the choice of God but rather of His people. At best, it was an external relationship, producing a mere surface

---

[16] 1st 5 books of Moses

knowledge *about* God. This evidence comes to us from the words, "the children of Israel knew his acts".

If we analyze the relationship between God and the children of Israel, we see it thoroughly frustrated God. At one point, so strained was the relationship between God and His People, that God threatened to produce a nation of descendants from the seed of Moses, rather than through the stubborn people, which at that time, made up the nation of Israel. We know that from a scripture, written by Moses in the book of Deuteronomy:

Deuteronomy 9:13-14
"Furthermore, YeHoVaH spoke unto me, saying, I have seen this people, and, behold, it is a stiff-necked people: Let me alone, that I may destroy them, and blot out their name from under heaven: and I will make of you a nation mightier and greater than they."

It is hard for us to fathom that anyone could frustrate God, but the plain truth of the matter is that God chose a specific people, whom He destined to be the nation with whom He dwelt in their midst. If that nation had received God's perfect will for them, they would *demonstrate the Divine Nature and plans of God for mankind to every other nation. From that demonstration, all peoples would know God's salvation message and from that point onward, know God as well.* This divine purpose, if obtained, found its fruitfulness as God's people knew God's ways and *adopted them* as their own. Instead, the Israelites chose to keep their own ways and do their own thing. What seems apparent is the fact that they tried to use God as a self-serving tool to meet their needs.

That is really the bottom line of God's frustration with Israel. From the scriptures, we hear God call them stiff-necked. Stiff-necked is a term that, over the centuries, conveys the idea of stubbornness, and while that shows its basic meaning, to obtain a biblical meaning of the word "stiff-necked", we need to understand that it is a condition of the heart. A stiff-necked person refuses, from their inner most being, to change their ways. It is not that they cannot change to do what is required of them, especially when God is there to help them. They simply refuse to change. Regarding the children of Israel, they needed to change their ways, to take on the ways of YeHoVaH.

Unfortunately, the children of Israel, for the most part, liked their own ways. If, on the other hand, they abandoned their own ways, then they would be a "holy" people unto God. This was the bottom line of the invitation God gave them:

Exodus 19: 5-6
"Now therefore, if you will obey my voice indeed, and keep my covenant, then you shall be a precious treasure unto me above all people: for all the earth is mine: And you shall be unto me a kingdom of priests, and a holy nation. These are the words which you shall speak unto the children of Israel."

Unfortunately, that stiff-necked condition of the children of Israel did not end after the five books of Moses but continued. Through the pages of the Bible, we read of Israelites who continually refused to exchange their thinking and their ways for God's mindset and behaviour. We read how they embraced whatever "gods" of the nations around them that they felt would satisfy their needs, give them what they thought they needed. They embraced and practised heathen rituals and traditions, which God strictly prohibited. These practices, their sins and their constant, stubborn refusal to repent, moved them far away from the call of God upon their lives. Yet, we hear, time after time, God calling to His people to return to Him[17]:

---

17 Bold & italics in the following scripture are not in the original texts.

Isaiah 44:22
"I have blotted out, as a thick cloud, your transgressions, and, as a cloud, your sins: return unto me; for I have redeemed you."

Jeremiah 4:1
"If you will return, O Israel, says YeHoVaH, return unto me: and if you will put away your abominations out of my sight, then shall you not remove."

Jeremiah 24:7
"And I will give them a heart to know me, that I am YeHoVaH: and they shall be my people, and I will be their God: for they shall return unto me with their whole heart."

Malachi 3:7
"Even from the days of your fathers you are gone away from my ordinances, and have not kept them. Return unto me, and I will return unto you, says YeHoVaH of hosts. But you said, Wherein shall we return?"

That cry fell on deaf hears, unchanging a people who continued to hold on to their own ways, refusing to accept the ways of God. If a student of the Word does a detailed study of First Covenant happenings, looking at God's desire and His people's response, it could be seen that they wanted God only under certain conditions, namely, under their own terms. God could provide for them food and shelter. He could allot them an inheritance in a promised land and increase their wealth, but they would not adopt God's call to look like Him in all their doings.

When in times of trouble, when they felt they needed help, they cried out to God. They desired a divine action to set them free from the oppressive circumstances in which they found themselves. Soon afterwards, however, they and their children forgot their commitment to serve God. It was external and not heartfelt. As we read through the First Covenant, we see that most of the children of Israel never desired to know their God like Moses knew Him. They were content only to be the recipients of His Acts, when and where they felt they needed them to manifest.

God gave them the Law, which included the 10 commandments, a pattern of living outlining behaviour towards God and man. It was to be a teacher instructing them and pointing out their sinfulness. It showed them their need for a Saviour. Instead, they broke the Law, continually.

Of course, this repeated behaviour, generation after generation, merited God's corrective attention. In God's eyes, He could not allow such behaviour to continue without addressing it. To God, their behaviour, which should draw others to their God, instead blasphemed His Holy Name:

Isaiah 52:5
"Now therefore, what have I here, says YeHoVaH, that my people is taken away for nought? they that rule over them make them to howl, says YeHoVaH; and my name continually every day is blasphemed."

2 Samuel 12:14
"Howbeit, because by this deed you have given great occasion to the enemies of YeHoVaH to blaspheme, the child also that is born unto you shall surely die."

Ezekiel 36:21-23
"But I had pity for my holy name, which the house of Israel had profaned among the heathen, wherever they went. Therefore say unto the house of Israel, Thus says the Lord YeHoVaH; I do not [this] for your sakes, O house of Israel, but for my holy name's sake, which you have profaned among the heathen, wherever you went. And I will sanctify my great name, which was profaned among the heathen, which you have profaned in the midst of them; and the heathen shall know that I [am] the YeHoVaH, says the Lord, YeHoVaH when I shall be sanctified in you before their eyes."

If we could take the time and do a detailed study of Biblical history, we would see that repeatedly the children of Israel embraced false gods, adopting heathen practices, including offering their children up in a sacrifice to a heathen God, Molech. We see their overall behaviour, as God saw it, profaned, and blasphemed the name of YeHoVaH. Yet, God's pleadings with the children of Israel met with continual, stiff-necked resistance. They kept their sin and continued to profane and blaspheme the name of their God.

CAN CHRISTIANS BLASPHEME GOD?

Paul, the Apostle, refers to blaspheming God. We find that in the letter to the Romans:

Romans 2:24
"For the name of God is blasphemed among the Gentiles through you, as it is written."

What does it mean to profane or blaspheme God's Name? Let's look at it in the Hebrew.

DEFINITIONS		
Blaspheme	Strong's # 5006	נאץ
		naw-ats
In Strong's, to blaspheme means to abhor, despise, or contemn.		
In the ancient picture language, we see portrayed the inheritance (life), vehemently put into a position that makes it vulnerable. In modern words, our inheritance is trampled under foot. That shows great		

despising, disrespecting, disregarding or spurning the things of God.

Profane	Strong's # 2490	חלל
		khaw-lal
It basically means to prostitute, to make common what God declares is holy.		
In the ancient picture language, it carries the picture of walling out the authority of God.		

In reflecting on God's heart in this matter, we see God's extended hand to Israel, inviting them to come and avail themselves of the same opportunity He gave to Moses: *to know His Ways*. Instead of doing that, they despised the things of YeHoVaH, and if we accept the meaning seen in the Hebraic Word picture, they trampled under foot their inheritance.

While Israel had an inheritance in the land, and also an inheritance of the Law given to them, they were also YeHoVaH's inheritance:

Deuteronomy 4:20
"But YeHoVaH has taken you, and brought you forth out of the iron furnace, even out of Egypt, to be unto him a people of inheritance, as you are this day."

In this passage we read that God took Israel unto Himself making them an inheritance for Himself. Israel, therefore, was God's inheritance. In other passages we read:

Deuteronomy 32:7-9
"Remember the days of old, consider the years of many generations: ask your father, and he will show you; your elders, and they will tell you. When the most High divided to the nations their inheritance, when he separated the sons of Adam, he set the bounds of the people according to the number of the children of Israel. For YeHoVaH's portion is his people; Jacob is the lot of his inheritance. He found him in a desert land, and in the waste howling wilderness; he led him about, he instructed him, he kept him as the apple of his eye. "For YeHoVaH's portion is his people; Jacob is the lot of his inheritance."

So, Israel is the inheritance of God, and in another scripture, we see where the Levitical priests were given a special inheritance too, that inheritance was God:

Deuteronomy 18:1-2
"The priests the Levites, and all the tribe of Levi, shall have no part nor inheritance with Israel: they shall eat the offerings of YeHoVaH made by fire, and his inheritance. Therefore, shall they have no inheritance among their brethren: YeHoVaH is their inheritance, as he has said unto them."

God is the inheritance of the priests. They were given no parcel of land within the allotted territories as an inheritance, as the other sons of Jacob received. This demonstrated that God, their inheritance, is of far greater value than a piece of property in the Promised land. It was God's design that the priests, as well as God's chosen people, respected their inheritance. Unfortunately, as we have just seen, they despised it.

A CHRISTIAN'S INHERITANCE
As Christians, we have a great inheritance:

1 Peter 1:3-5
"Blessed be the God and Father of our Lord Jesus Christ, which according to his abundant mercy has begotten us again unto a lively hope by the resurrection of Jesus Christ from the dead, To an inheritance incorruptible, and undefiled, and that fades not away, reserved in heaven for you, Who are kept by the power of God through faith unto salvation ready to be revealed in the last time."

Can believers blaspheme (show disrespect, distain, trample under foot) that inheritance? On that topic the scripture says:

1 Peter 1:3-5
"Blessed be the God and Father of our Lord Jesus Christ, which according to his abundant mercy has begotten us again unto a lively hope by the resurrection of Jesus Christ

from the dead, To an inheritance incorruptible, and undefiled, and that fades not away, reserved in heaven for you, Who are kept by the power of God through faith unto salvation ready to be revealed in the last time."

It goes without saying that Yeshua, the Son of God, is a valuable treasure, as is the precious blood which He shed for our sins. Through His self-less act on the cross of Calvary, He obtained for us an imperishable inheritance, which has secured for us all blessings in heavenly places[18]. Yet, in the passage we just read, according to the book of Hebrews, it is possible to trample under foot the Son of God and count the blood of the covenant wherever we were set apart to God, as an unholy thing, and has done to despite (given insult) to the Spirit of grace.

CHAPTER'S SUMMARY
As we walked together through this chapter, we discussed the open invitation of God to His People to come to Him. That invitation was to know Him, not just about Him. We saw that God desired His people to change their behaviour so that they would be holy, and as such, reflect His image to the nations around them. Instead, we saw that they profaned and blasphemed God's Name.

---

[18] *Ephesians 1:3 Blessed be the God and Father of our Lord Jesus Christ, who has blessed us with all spiritual blessings in heavenly places in Christ:*

In addition, it was stated that if we had time to do a detailed study, we could easily see that the children of Israel wanted God to meet their needs. To put this in modern terms we might understand today: they desired God to enable them to receive the desires of their heart, but they were not willing to adjust those desires to align with God's desires for them. They were not willing to embrace God's Ways, but rather desired to use God for a means to their own ends.

So, the question remains, do Christians today do the same thing as the ancient Israelites? Let's not assess overall Christianity here, rather take it to a personal level and ask these questions thoughtfully and prayerfully before God. *(While the book calls for a yes or no answer, if you so desire, go deeper and write out more on a piece of paper, or in your workbook.)*

**Let's ensure, as we pursue God,
that we do not seek Him only for His acts.
Let's pursue God to know and
adopt His Ways for our life.**

For those readers without the workbook, who might want to talk with God about this matter, here is a simple 6 question chart. Consider taking this chart to your prayer times, discussing the questions and answers with God.

AM I ANY DIFFERENT[19] THAN ISRAEL IN ANCIENT TIMES?

Question	Yes/No
Do I expect God to meet my needs and do it on my terms?	
Are my prayers demanding, focused only what I need or think important?	
Am I "stiff-necked" in God's eyes in any of my dealings with God?	
Do I perceive God as the Bible teaches, or as I desire to see Him?	
Do I give God the desires of my heart so He can adjust them to His desires?	
Do I sincerely and whole-heartedly want to know God, or do I only want to know His Acts?	

---

[19] Chart also in your workbook, with additional space for information.

WHEN ENCOUNTERING GOD'S AUTHORITY

3

"For ever, YeHoVaH, your word is settled in heaven."
Psalm 119:89

*I*N THE ABOVE scripture, the Hebrew word, interpreted in English as the word "settled", carries with it the idea of something firmly established, unchangeable, standing erect forever. God, therefore, makes it very clear that His Word is the last word, and it is unmovable. It is the ultimate authority. Considering that, Christian believers need to understand what it means to live our lives under the mantle of God's ultimate authority.

To understand God's Ultimate authority, let's first define the word, "authority". One online dictionary defines authority as "the right to command or to act; or power exercised by a person in virtue of his office or trust" [20]. To shorten that definition to fit in with today's lingo, we might sum up the meaning of "authority" as "the final word". In reference to God's Word, to agree with what God, Himself, says about His Word, we must add a few more words and say that God's authority is the last word *with an unalterable impact*. That agrees with what the opening Psalm in this chapter states:

Psalm 119:89
"For ever, YeHoVaH, your word is settled in heaven."

What do we know today about ultimate authority? In the world in which we live, do we have any living examples of such authority?

As we assess some facts in our overall society, we find that parental authority, as naturally given by God, more often than not, is challenged by the couple's children. Many parents, under pressure from a child's convincing tears or words, allow themselves to be worn down by their child's behaviour. If parents give in to their child's demands, they weaken their authority with that child and inadvertently, teach their

---

[20] Webster's online dictionary

child, that their authority is not the final word. It is negotiable.

Do parents, in our society today, really grasp the far distant ramifications of such behaviour in a child's life, who constantly has others cater to their demands, who never learns the meaning of the word, "no"? Will these behaviours, embed in the child's mind, and carry over to manipulate other authorities they encounter in their lifetime? How does such learned behavior impact the child's adult life? What many parents do not understand is that the mindsets they forge, even accidentally, in their child's mind forms a foundation for a lifetime, a place from which they make their choices.

Continual, and extreme leniency implemented when raising children, which constantly gives in to self-centered demands, fails to set in place positive parameters for the child. Child rearing practices that do not establish safe parameters and help a child develop self-control and respect for others, including authority figures, become a danger. This silently teaches children to challenge other authority figures such as teachers or officers of the law, the courts systems, etc.

As we listen to news media reports in our present society, we hear of incidents where some schools are no longer a place of safety for students or teachers. Some have been invaded by perpetrators who have wounded, and even killed, students and teachers. News reporters bring horror stories of churches, too, that are not safe, as some pastors and even parishioners are shot while attending a service. Some churches, to keep their church a safe place, have implemented armed security guards, in plain clothes, to monitor church gatherings.

In assessing our air waves today, we see they are constantly bombarded by a barrage of reports that portray great disrespect for officers of the law. Even court judges have their authority challenged, for which offenders receive a conviction of contempt of court, yet even that conviction might be appealed. Our society, which has been coined as a free-thinking society, has been known to adjust its behaviour codes in such a way as to point a finger at certain linear standards, dismissing the former rules as prejudice. Is it possible that the base of this kind of revolution, which occurs slowly over decades, is a philosophy, "whatever feels good, do it"?

Unfortunately, that increase of these things in our society, has also crept into Christian churches. Some preachers treat the Word of God as an allegory. Others treat it is an archaic, narrow-minded tool, not applicable today. Some look at the Word of God as an historic book, an example of ancient literature but with no more emphasis than any other book. They laugh if suggested it is used as a guide for modern society today. To many people, even within the church setting, to say God's Word is the ultimate authority invites debate on your opinion verses mine.

Overall, then, in our general society, it is probably safe to say that we rarely see authority implemented as a final word, with an unchangeable impact. Such authority is, therefore, hard to grasp. Even so, while this may well be true, to those who hold to Judean-Christian principles of the faith, our life must be different. We must embrace the Bible as the last word, one with unchanging parameters. We must recognize its principles as truth and therefore align our life with those truths.

Regarding God, a Christian believer's behaviour is plainly stated, as we see in the following verses:

Deuteronomy 6:5
"And you shall love YeHoVaH your God with all your heart, and with all your soul, and with all your might."

Deuteronomy 30:16
"In that I command you this day to love YeHoVaH your God, to walk in his ways, and to keep his commandments and his statutes and his judgments, that you may live and

multiply: and YeHoVaH your God shall bless you in the land where you go to possess it."

First, comes the love for God, which is not a surface love, but embraces the entire being of the believer. Then comes the behaviour which results from that love, namely, walking in all His ways, keeping God's commandments, statutes, and His judgments.

God does not stop by telling us only how to love and serve Him, He gives us information on how to treat our fellow man. This Yeshua reaffirmed and summarized:

Matthew 22:37-40
"Jesus said unto him, you shall love YeHoVaH your God with all your heart, and with all your soul, and with all your mind. This is the first and great commandment. And the second is like unto it, you shall love your neighbour as yourself. On these two commandments hang all the law and the prophets."

For the serious, dedicated Christian, there is no compromise on these behavioural commands to love our God with all our being and love our neighbour with the same love we have for ourselves. God's Word, outlining our behaviour, beyond a shadow of a doubt, must be embraced. Therefore, the questions that committed Christians should ask is not "about the validity of authority of the Word of God," but rather, how does knowing that fact impact our personal Christian life?

In other words, the committed Christian, determined to please YeHoVaH, looks at ways that they should alter their life, to adjust to the demands of the Word of God, and not the other way around, learning how they can alter the Word, to fit their chosen lifestyle. One example of necessary life changes, after a commitment to become a Christian, is that of a former thief, who wants to walk within the faith. Their prior behaviour must be adjusted to align with the command of YeHoVaH, "you shall not steal"[21].

That former example is an obvious example, but we see less obvious examples everyday in our churches, which do not result in realigned living parameters. For example, how many people make verbal commitments to follow the Christian way and while they may stay away from what they think are the "big sins" in life, they overlook what they classify as little things. Perhaps, under certain circumstances they think, it is alright to lie, sneak out past parental curfew, cheat on exams or later in life, cheat on how they record their income for taxes. To some, it is not a big thing to speak all manner of evil against their neighbour, making

---

[21] Exodus 20:15

jokes about their character, which ends up being a character slam or assassination.

To others it is not a problem if they hit another's car in a parking lot and walk away without any note to inform the owner of the dinted car how they can be contacted to repair the vehicle. What about those who excuse looking at porno magazines, movies, or websites? The list goes on and on of everyday things that a professing Christian *might do*, things that they see others do. Their friends or others they know declare such and such a behaviour is OK because everyone does it. Consideration for God's Word, as the ultimate authority, may declare that action offensive, but good excuses seem to take precedence.

What is the bottom-line of all these things? Is it that the church opened its door to the philosophies of the world and embraced them as their own? Is it a result of free-thinking society's influence on church leaders and members alike? Is it an attempt to squeeze Christianity into a mould, to present the faith more acceptable to others and thus obtain new converts? All these things may weigh out as important factors, but is it possible that Christians, somewhere along the line, lost respect and reverence for the Word of God and therefore, not only challenged God's ultimate authority in their life, but watered down His principles to fit in with their mindset?

If Christians really desire to embrace the Word of God as God instructs them to do, they must recognize, first, that it is the ultimate authority of the Living God to Whom we give account, and secondly, they must implement whatever changes are necessary to align their lives with that authority. For the serious, committed believer, this is the bottom line. For anyone struggling in this regard, it is imperative to take time with YeHoVaH and bring forward any doubts, any excuses one might use to object to such embracing of God's Word and the alignment that follows.

There are questions in the workbook to help in that matter, as well as scriptures in this chapter, to help the reader recognize the treasure that we have, even the benefits of establishing God's Word as the ultimate authority by which we measure and then align our lives.

God's Word, like His character, is constant and unchanging!

UNCHANGEABLE CHARACTER OF GOD

Exodus 34:6
"And YeHoVaH passed by before him, and proclaimed, YeHoVaH, YeHoVaH God, merciful and gracious, longsuffering, and abundant in goodness and truth."

Deuteronomy 32: 4
"He is the Rock, his work is perfect: for all his ways are judgment: a God of truth and without iniquity, just and right is he."

Psalm 33:4
"For the word of YeHoVaH is right; and all his works are done in truth."

Psalm 43:3
"O send out your light and your truth: let them lead me; let them bring me unto your holy hill, and to your tabernacles."

Psalm 57:10
"For your mercy is great unto the heavens, and your truth unto the clouds."

Psalm 100:5
"For YeHoVaH is good; his mercy is everlasting; and his truth endures to all generations."

Psalm 108: 4
"For your mercy is great above the heavens: and your truth reaches unto the clouds."

Psalm 119:142
"Your righteousness is an everlasting righteousness, and your law is the truth."

Psalm 119:151
"You are near, YeHoVaH; and all your commandments are truth."

Psalm 25:10
"All the paths of YeHoVaH are mercy and truth unto such as keep his covenant and his testimonies."

ABOUT ADDING TO GOD'S WORD

Proverbs 30:5-6
"Every word of God [is] pure: he [is] a shield unto them that put their trust in him. Add thou not unto his words, lest he reprove thee, and thou be found a liar."

Deuteronomy 4:2
"You shall not add unto the word which I command you, neither shall you diminish [ought] from it, that you may keep the commandments of YeHoVaH your God which I command you."

ABOUT BENEFITS OF GOD'S WORD[22]

Psalm 119:138
"Your testimonies [that] you have commanded [are] righteous and very faithful."

---

[22] These are from Psalm 119 but there are many more within the Old and Second Covenant.

Psalm 119:98
"You through your commandments have made me wiser than my enemies: for they [are] ever with me."

Psalm 119:128
"Therefore I esteem all [your] precepts [concerning] all [things to be] right; [and] I hate every false way."

Psalm 119:54
"Your statutes have been my songs in the house of my pilgrimage."

Psalm 119:11
"Your word have I hid in my heart, that I might not sin against thee."

Psalm 119:105
"Your word is a lamp unto my feet, and a light unto my path."

Psalm 119:140
"Your word is very pure: therefore your servant loves it."

Psalm 119: 160
"Your word is true from the beginning: and every one of your righteous judgments endures for ever."

One other scripture to consider, to which many more could be added:

GOD'S COURT OF LAW

Psalm 89: 14
"Justice and judgment are the habitation of your throne: mercy and truth shall go before your face."

Many more scriptures speak of the practices commanded in Word of God, encouraging believers to be strict adherents to it. Numerous scriptures give reasons why we should desire to follow it and not to make our own way by departing from the path God illuminates for us in His Word. God's Word holds, for the serious Christian believer, good advice, as each precept, law, testimony, or command uttered, manifests for the protection of those who wish to live a godly, pleasing life, before the eyes of YeHoVaH.

Fellow mankind, including other Christian believers, might not like the way in which Bible-based, Bible-believing Christians live out their life, but nevertheless, the measuring stick of obedience to God cannot be the opinions of the society in which we live or even the opinions of other Christian believers. God's Word and God's Word alone must be the ultimate authority in a believer's life. Living our live as such may cause persecution, verbal and otherwise, but we are not the first generation to face that reaction.

In fact, we can read advice given by Paul to his son in the faith, Titus, as a response to happenings in the first century:

Titus 2:1-15
"But speak the things which become sound doctrine: That the aged men be sober, grave, temperate, sound in faith, in charity, in patience. The aged women likewise, that they be in behaviour as becomes holiness, not false accusers, not given to much wine, teachers of good things; That they may teach the young women to be sober, to love their husbands, to love their children, To be discreet, chaste, keepers at home, good, obedient to their own husbands, that the word of God be not blasphemed. Young men likewise exhort to be sober minded. In all things showing yourself a pattern of good works: in doctrine showing uncorruptness, gravity, sincerity, 8 Sound speech, that cannot be condemned; that he that is of the contrary part may be ashamed, having no evil thing to say of you.

Exhort servants to be obedient unto their own masters, and to please them well in all things; not answering again; Not misappropriating but showing all good faithfulness; that they may adorn the doctrine of God our Saviour in all things. For the grace of God that brings salvation has appeared to all men, Teaching us that, denying ungodliness and worldly lusts, we should live soberly, righteously, and godly, in this present world; Looking for that blessed hope, and the glorious appearing of the great God and our Saviour Jesus

Christ; Who gave himself for us, that he might redeem us from all iniquity, and purify unto himself a precious people, zealous of good works. These things speak, and exhort, and rebuke with all authority. Let no man despise you."

As scripture above speaks of advice to the believer, verse 12 and 13 basically recap the lifestyle God desires for the Second Covenant believer, showing us that the grace of God teaches us much. Believers should not live for ungodliness nor worldly lusts.

Rather, believers need to live soberly, which is King James English for "controlling, through the power of the Holy Spirit, one's desires and impulses, so they live by the power of the Spirit and not of the flesh." Each believer should live by God's standard of righteousness, living in a way that God approves. Furthermore, any longings should shift from things of this world, which have no eternal value, to consider wisely the things of the Kingdom of God, including the promise of Yeshua's return to this earth.

Living as the Apostle Paul stated in Titus, and as he and other inspired writers stated in the New Testament, will help believers to see the Hand of God move within their own life and beyond their church walls. If summarized, the New Testament message projects a pattern for each believer who claims the name of Yeshua as "Lord", ensuring He rules over every aspect of our life, and "Master", in that we live for Him and Him alone.

CHAPTER'S SUMMARY:
For the Christian, God's Word must be the Ultimate Authority on which we base our entire faith system, and the life we live, here upon the earth. The serious believer knows that compromising on God's Word, in application to any aspect of our life, will never produce God's intended fruit. Dedicated Christians will use the Word of God as a benchmark for their thinking, behaviour, and life's responses, longing to please YeHoVaH in all their ways.

As we looked at Titus 2, we noted verse 12 and 13 teaches us to focus on godly behaviour, living in righteousness for God, in this present world, with our eyes upon the blessed hope and the glorious appearing of our Saviour. This form of behaviour suited well the believers of that time, when the early, New Testament church experienced growing pains, as well as much affliction. It remains good advice for believers today.

**Let each serious believer ensure that the
Ultimate Authority of God
forms the foundation of their life!**

CHAPTER 4 INTRO

This next chapter looks at the importance of a proper faith foundation. While, in this book, we discuss God's intentions for His children to stand upon a firm, solid faith foundation, one that He specifically established for believers in the Second Covenant, *we do not discuss specific fundamental aspects of the Christian faith.*

However, in the interest of common ground, to help the reader to understand some comments of the author, you will find an inclusion of *the author's faith* statement of fundamental beliefs in the back of your workbook[23]. This faith statement is evangelical in its base, and therefore, common with most evangelical believers.

Whether you agree or disagree with the faith statement, at least you will know the basis on which the author places her beliefs. Again, that is the reason for its inclusion.

---

[23] If you did not obtain the Workbook, go to Cegullah Publishing's website, and read the faith statement. It is the same as in the workbook. www.cegullapublishing.ca/faith-statement/

WHEN ACCEPTING GOD'S FOUNDATION

4

"Now therefore you are no more strangers and foreigners, but fellow citizens with the saints, and of the household of God; And are built upon the foundation of the apostles and prophets, Jesus Christ himself being the chief corner stone."
Ephesians 2:19-20

*P*AUL, THE APOSTLE, in writing to the Gentile church at Ephesus, instructed these converts to remember that they were no longer strangers, foreigners, or in modern term, "outsiders" to God's household, but rather, they were fellow citizens with the other saints, those of Jewish origin, as well as Gentile believers elsewhere. This is just one passage where Paul speaks of the oneness of the Jew and

Gentile, as God brought them together as one in His Only Son, Yeshua. Gentiles, converted to Messiah, now enjoyed a foundation built upon the apostles and prophets, and of course, the cornerstone of God's building, Yeshua, the same as converted Jews.

As the scripture continued to unfold its message, it further describes the spiritual building:

Ephesians 2:21-22
"In whom all the building fitly framed together grows unto a holy temple in YeHoVaH: In whom you also are built together for a habitation of God through the Spirit."

At the time when the Apostle, Paul, wrote the book of Ephesians, the Jews had a beautiful temple in Jerusalem. This was not Solomon's temple, since Nebuchadnezzar's army destroyed it many centuries before Messiah came. No, the temple standing in Jerusalem at the time when Paul penned this epistle, was different. Looking at history, we see that after the Jews returned from Babylon, they built another temple. It was very simple and very plain. However, King Herod, in 19 B.C.E., to be accepted by the Jews, had the temple rebuilt, dressing it up with precious metals such as silver, gold and the like. Levitical priests supervised the temple's take down, expanding its platform and rebuilding its inner and outer chambers. Even prior to the Temple being finished, around 63 A.D., it was considered one of the seven wonders of the world.

As we consider Paul's letter to the Gentile believers at Ephesus, we must remember they too had a beautiful temple. It was dedicated to the goddess Diana. That temple was also so elaborate that, it too, was one of the seven wonders of the world at that time. Obviously, Gentile believers in Ephesus would not populate the pagan temple there. In the Covenant springing forth from Messiah's sacrifice, no temple, not even the one at Jerusalem dedicated to the God of Abraham, Isaac and Jacob would become the focus of believers in Messiah. In the book of Acts, as the apostles and other disciples went up to the Temple at the hour of prayer, their focus was not on the importance of the Temple but was rather on prayer and the fulfill YeHoVaH's command to share the gospel, beginning at Jerusalem:

Luke 24:44-49
"And he said unto them, These are the words which I spoke unto you, while I was yet with you, that all things must be fulfilled, which were written in the law of Moses, and in the prophets, and in the psalms, concerning me. Then opened he their understanding, that they might understand the scriptures, And said unto them, Thus it is written, and thus it was right for Christ to suffer, and to rise from the dead the third day: And that repentance and remission of sins should be preached in his name among all nations, beginning at

Jerusalem. And you are witnesses of these things. And, behold, I send the promise of my Father upon you: but tarry in the city of Jerusalem, until you be endued with power from on high."

Regarding the temple at Jerusalem, the book of Hebrews clearly tells us that the only temple, which Christians need concern themselves, is *not* that temple erected in Jerusalem, nor of its high priests, or its sacrifices, but rather, is a heavenly temple, the very one Yeshua entered:

Hebrews 9:1-10
"Then truly the first [covenant] had also ordinances of divine service, and a worldly sanctuary. For there was a tabernacle made; the first, wherein [was] the menorah, and the table, and the showbread; which is called the sanctuary. And after the second veil, the tabernacle which is called the Holiest of all; Which had the golden censer, and the ark of the covenant overlaid round about with gold, wherein [was] the golden pot that had manna, and Aaron's rod that budded, and the tables of the covenant; And over it the cherubims of glory shadowing the mercy seat; of which we cannot now speak particularly. "

"Now when these things were thus ordained, the priests went always into the first tabernacle, accomplishing the service [of God]. But into the second [went] the high priest alone once every year, not without blood, which he offered

for himself, and [for] the errors of the people: The Holy Ghost this signifying, that the way into the holiest of all was not yet made manifest, while as the first tabernacle was yet standing: Which [was] a figure for the time then present, in which were offered both gifts and sacrifices, that could not make him that did the service perfect, as pertaining to the conscience; [Which stood] only in meats and drinks, and divers washings, and carnal ordinances, imposed [on them] until the time of reformation."

This heavenly tabernacle, into which Yeshua entered, human hands did not make, like the Temple on earth. That earthly temple was a mere type, a representation, a prophetic picture of the real Tabernacle in heaven. Likewise, the sacrifices offered foreshadowed, typed, or prefigured, Yeshua. Thus, scripture makes it clear, these things existed until after Yeshua's death, burial, resurrection, and ascension into heaven, until, what the scripture calls, the time of reformation. After that time, these things served no purpose. No longer were they necessary.

To believers, in the early church, especially those of Jewish origin, getting used to the idea that, neither the Temple nor its sacrifices, were necessary any longer, would take some thinking and behavioural changes. A reformation is a time of changing or bringing in a behavioural adjustment. In the passage where we read of the time of reformation, the author used the Greek word, διόρθωσις[24]. It means to thoroughly straighten something that is out of alignment.

Reflecting on Paul's words, "until the time of reformation", we see his reasoning. Looking at the temple, with its rituals and sacrifices foreshadowing or prophetically demonstrating Yeshua, once Yeshua came, the need for these things no longer existed. Realignment is now necessary to shift a believer's thinking from a First Covenant mindset, which foreshadowed or promised Messiah, to a new mindset, which declares that Yeshua came. Hence, the words, "the time of reformation". Yeshua, the fulfillment of the First Covenant, invites believers then, to live in the light of His coming, and that means a shift of focus in many ways, among them, thoughts of a heavenly Temple.

Having that focus clear in our minds, let us return to the theme in our opening scripture in this chapter:

Ephesians 2:19-20
"Now therefore you are no more strangers and foreigners, but fellow citizens with the saints, and of the household of God; And are built upon the foundation of the apostles and prophets, Jesus Christ himself being the chief corner stone;"

---

[24] Strong's #1357 διόρθωσις (pronounced dee-or'-tho-sis). Sourced from onlinebible.net.

If we follow through with this comparison of Yeshua's followers to the idea of a temple, a spiritual temple, we see that the cumulative members of the first century church, each are built upon the foundation of the apostles and prophets, with Yeshua as the chief cornerstone. It is this theme, to which we'll devout this chapter.

A CORNERSTONE AND ITS PURPOSE
In ancient days, when erecting a building, since they did not have the technology that we have today, they took lines very slow and easy in building. Normally, they would ensure the ground was as level as possible and then, they'd take great care to ensure the cornerstone was properly placed. It must be 100 percent accurate. If not, the whole building would be out of alignment. Then, from that perfectly seated cornerstone, they would place the foundation stones, ensuring each one measured against the cornerstone. After the foundation was in perfect alignment, then they added the other stones to create a solid building to stand the test of time.

Yeshua is the cornerstone of the Christian faith. We know this from several scriptures. First, let's look at Isaiah, which spoke of the cornerstone:

Isaiah 28:16
"Therefore thus says the Lord YeHoVaH, Behold, I lay in Zion for a foundation a stone, a tried stone, a precious corner [stone], a sure foundation: he that believes shall not make haste."

In the book of Psalms, we find another mention of a cornerstone, a rejected cornerstone, which God made chief stone:

Psalm 118:22
"The stone which the builders refused is become the head stone of the corner."

In the gospels, we hear that Yeshua identified Himself as the fulfillment of that prophecy:

Matthew 21:42-44
"Jesus said unto them, Did you never read in the scriptures, The stone which the builders rejected, the same is become the head of the corner: this is YeHoVaH's doing, and it is marvellous in our eyes? Therefore say I unto you, The kingdom of God shall be taken from you, and given to a nation bringing forth the fruits thereof. And whosoever shall fall on this stone shall be broken: but on whomsoever it shall fall, it will grind him to powder."

Yeshua, then, is the stone the builder's rejected, referring to the Jewish leaders at that time, but

YeHoVaH took that same stone and made it the head of the corner, or the cornerstone. From that perfectly seated cornerstone, the building work continues to position the foundation. In a spiritual sense, the teachings and the prophets comprise the foundation stones. Prophets, including Moses, foretold of Yeshua.

Looking at their writings, with an understanding of its revelation of Yeshua, we strengthen our faith knowing Yeshua to be the fulfillment. Apostles Yeshua chose to bear His message, speak not just of Yeshua as the fulfillment of the First Covenant, but also outline Apostolic doctrines which centre on Yeshua.

YESHUA IN SCRIPTURE

John 5:39
"Search the scriptures; for in them you think you have eternal life: and they are they which testify of me".

John 5:46
"For had you believed Moses, you would have believed me: for he wrote of me."

Both these scriptures, uttered by Yeshua, state that scripture speaks of Him. As the Prophets foretold of the Promised Messiah, they described him, giving clues to his identity, yet the complete picture of the Messiah lay hidden within the First Covenant.

Those living under the First Covenant did not understand the complete picture, and even during the time when Yeshua came and spoke with Israel, they did not understand that the very fulfillment of scripture stood in front of them. It was not until after the death, burial and resurrection of Yeshua took place, that the Apostle's completely understood. That understanding did not suddenly come either. It took a specific action of Yeshua:

Luke 24:44-48
"And he said unto them, These are the words which I spoke unto you, while I was yet with you, that all things must be fulfilled, which were written in the law of Moses, and in the prophets, and in the psalms, concerning me. Then opened he their understanding25, that they might understand the scriptures, And said unto them, Thus it is written, and thus it was right that Christ suffer, and to rise from the dead the third day: And that repentance and remission of sins should be preached in his name among all nations, beginning at Jerusalem. And you are witnesses of these things."

Yeshua opened their understanding to help them grasp that the Messiah was to suffer, to rise from the dead on the third day. Even though Yeshua prophesied to His disciples about His crucifixion and resurrection, they simply did not get it. Only after the

---

[25] Bolding and highlights are the author's.

fulfillment of prophecy, after Yeshua opened their understanding, did they grasp it. Yeshua was *concealed* in the First Covenant but revealed in the Second Covenant.

A good way to look at it is this way: Let's say, the records regarding the Messiah, were not written on parchment but rather puzzle format, with interlocking edges. God's People studied the puzzle pieces to assemble them, spreading them out on a large table in front of them. Some pieces easily fit together so scholars of the Word knew the intended birthplace of the Messiah, the lineage, and also an approximate timeframe, but other pieces, no matter how hard they tried, did not seem to fit.

If only this puzzle came with a picture to follow? Then, it would be easier! Generation, after generation, the scholars came together to understand the puzzle pattern, but they could not. Here a piece fit, and there a piece fit, but their minds were darkened as to its picture.

Suddenly, Yeshua comes. After His death, burial, and resurrection, He opens the disciple's minds. They get it! Yeshua is the picture the scholars wished they had earlier. He is the box lid, if you will, with the finished picture clearly displayed. With this picture in hand, now the puzzle pieces fit together quickly. They have the picture of the Messiah because they understand the earlier puzzle pieces.

For believers today, as we see the First Covenant, we see it with Yeshua as its fulfillment, and as we look at the Second Covenant, we see how the Old was revealed. We also know that each teaching we receive should uplift Yeshua, showing Him as God revealed Him! Yeshua, as He came, showed that He was the long-awaited Messiah, but also, He gave us a clear picture of something perceived blurry, as the puzzle pieces fit together: the image of God.

Hebrews 1:3
"Who being the brightness of his glory, and the exact image of his person, and upholding all things by the word of his power, when he had by himself purged our sins, sat down on the right hand of the Majesty on high;"

Here, the words "exact image" presents the idea of a stamped image. Interpreted to modern English, this scripture means that Yeshua showed us God, Who Yeshua addressed, as do we, "Father". "Upholding all things by the word of His power" emphasizes His oneness in the Godhead, for Who but God could do such at thing! That passage certainly speaks of Yeshua, for it tells us that after He removed the sin of the world, He sat down at the Father's right hand.

ANOTHER REVEALED IMAGE

Summarizing what we've discussed thus far, Yeshua is the cornerstone, the prophets, and apostles the foundation, all of which point to Yeshua. From that undergirding now, the other stones now sit. Believers are those stones. Each one fits together, and it follows through they will also point to Yeshua with their lifestyle, their words and service unto God, and reveal His image to others.

The question each believer must ask then is twofold:

> 1. Does everything I believe centre on Yeshua?
> 2. Do I reveal Yeshua to others?

This twofold question is not really a new question. Paul, the Apostle, in his address to the church, numerous times, spoke out against things people embraced that were not properly applied to Second Covenant style living, that did not shift into Second Covenant thinking. Below is an excerpt from Galatians which addressed an issue of justification coming by the Law, rather than by faith in Yeshua:

Galatians 5:4-9
"Christ is become of no effect unto you, whosoever of you are justified by the law; you are fallen from grace. For we

through the Spirit wait for the hope of righteousness by faith. For in Jesus Christ neither circumcision avails any thing, nor uncircumcision; but faith which works by love. You did run well; who did hinder you that you should not obey the truth? This persuasion comes not of him that called you. A little leaven leavens the whole lump."

In this passage, Paul addresses Second Covenant believers, who failed to shift from First Covenant thinking to that of the Second who focused on the circumcision for justification, under the Law, rather than being justified by faith in Yeshua. He clearly says they are hindered and do not obey the truth. Paul sees that return to the First Covenant as very dangerous and goes so far as to call their persuasion (doctrine) "not of God." Then, he compares their wrong doctrine to "leaven" which eventually enters the complete lump of dough.

Yeshua, Himself, in the book of Revelation, rebuked wrong doctrines embraced by Second Covenant believers because they formed stumbling stones for believers:

Revelation 2: 12-17
"And to the angel of the church in Pergamos write; These things says he which has the sharp sword with two edges; I know your works, and where you dwell, even where ha satan's seat is: and you hold fast my name, and have not

denied my faith, even in those days wherein Antipas was my faithful martyr, who was slain among you, where ha satan dwells. But I have a few things against you, because you have there them that hold the doctrine of Balaam, who taught Balac to cast a stumblingblock before the children of Israel, to eat things sacrificed unto idols, and to commit fornication. So you have also them that hold the doctrine of the Nicolaitans, which thing I hate. Repent; or else I will come unto you quickly and will fight against them with the sword of my mouth. He that has an ear, let him hear what the Spirit says unto the churches; To him that overcomes will I give to eat of the hidden manna, and will give him a white stone, and in the stone a new name written, which no man knows saving he that receives it."

Yeshua, after the cross, in a Word given to the Apostle John, speaks strongly against wrong doctrines, as they present stumbling blocks. Stumbling blocks cause people to trip over them. Earlier, while on earth, He spoke to His Disciples about the "leaven of wrong doctrine".

Matthew 16:11-12
"How is it that you do not understand that I spake it not to you concerning bread, that you should beware of the leaven of the Pharisees and of the Sadducees? Then understood they how that he bid them not beware of the leaven of bread, but of the doctrine of the Pharisees and of the Sadducees."

These two scriptures, from Revelation and Matthew, were not the only occasions when Yeshua spoke of the dangers of wrong doctrine. In the following scripture passage, Yeshua quoted a First Covenant prophet:

Isaiah 29:13
"Wherefore YeHoVaH said, Forasmuch as this people draw near [me] with their mouth, and with their lips do honour me, but have removed their heart far from me, and their fear toward me is taught by the precept of men."

Matthew 15:8-9
"This people draw near unto me with their mouth and honour me with [their] lips; but their heart is far from me. 9 But in vain they do worship me, teaching [for] doctrines the commandments of men."

It is not hard to conclude that additional doctrines, teachings, and practices of the faith are dangerous. No matter how good they sound, *if they do not align with the cornerstone, Yeshua, and do not agree with the foundation formed by the prophets and apostles*, they cause stumbling blocks, or act like leaven that goes through the entire lump of dough. This produces a result far below what God intended! Believers must watch, therefore, what they receive as teachings from God's Word. They are the ones who must examine closely to ensure that everything they believe aligns with the Word of God *in the way God intended*, not pulled out of context to suit a certain generation, a certain culture, or a certain mindset. Just as the Bible shows a picture of Yeshua, all doctrine should point to Him, and the picture believers represent must look like, sound like, express actions like Yeshua.

CHAPTER'S SUMMARY

This lesson presented the Second Covenant revelation of God's people as His spiritual Temple, and of the cornerstone, Yeshua. We looked at the necessity of accepting God's foundation as He established it for us. We saw that we must align, first with the cornerstone, and then ensure every part of our faith system aligns with it, meaning that every foundation stone, the writings of the prophets and apostles, refer to the cornerstone, Yeshua. We concluded this chapter with statements by the Apostle Paul, and Yeshua that spoke of the detrimental effects of wrong doctrine.

SOME PERSONAL QUESTIONS

To fully understand the complete alignment of our foundation and cornerstone, you're invited to analyze everything you believe and practice, both inside and outside of the assembly of believers. Below, you'll find two questions to prayerfully consider and investigate with YeHoVaH. Each one takes time and diligence to examine so don't expect the answers in an instant:

> YeHoVaH:
> Do I believe what the early, 1st century church believed?
> Do I hold added layers of teachings, theologies, practices, or rituals compiled from a later date?

To begin to answer these questions, consider making a detailed list of the many things you do daily, based on your daily habits. Include prayer times, spiritual as well as non-spiritual rituals which you do both inside and outside of church. [26] Then, read the New Testament, gospel and epistles, numerous times. Don't look to form theories, or support those you might hold as true. As you read, allow the Word to do its job of separating truth from error[27].

Also, ask YeHoVaH to help you look for specific instructions of *faith practices* for believers, as well as what they were told to avoid. Next, compare the list you made of habits, rituals, etc. Then, look to see how your behaviour matches up. This is just a place to begin. If you desire to do a faith audit, look for books to help you in that regard. Whatever you do, pray

---

[26] You might find it easier to do a journal, recording everyday events for one week. Perhaps think ahead to see if these are routine, and for those days (during a month, a year, etc.) when you celebrate religious events, record what they are how you celebrate them.

[27] *Hebrews 4:12-13*

every step of the way for God to help you carefully look at your foundation to assure it is what He laid out for His children to hold dear.

With God's help, let us assure our heart remains stedfast in God and our fear towards Him comes not by the precept of men[28]

---

[28] *Isaiah 29:13; Matthew 15:8-9*

WHEN RECOGNIZING GOD'S MIGHT

5

"YeHoVaH your God in the midst of you is mighty; he will save, he will rejoice over you with joy; he will rest in his love, he will joy over you with singing. I will gather them that are sorrowful for the solemn assembly, who are of you, to whom the reproach of it was a burden."
Zephaniah 3:17-18

*I*N BEGINNING THIS chapter, let's take a moment and listen to the Apostle, Peter, as he spoke to believers in the first century church.

2 Peter 1:1-4
" Simon Peter, a servant and an apostle of Jesus Christ, to them that have obtained like precious faith with us through

the righteousness of God and our Saviour Jesus Christ: Grace and peace be multiplied unto you through the knowledge of God, and of Jesus our Lord, According as his divine power has given unto us all things that pertain unto life and godliness, through the knowledge of him that has called us to glory and virtue: Whereby are given unto us exceeding great and precious promises: that by these you might be partakers of the divine nature, having escaped the corruption that is in the world through lust."

We know this message is to believers since Peter says in the opening part of this passage, "to them that have obtained like precious faith with us through the righteousness of God and our Saviour Jesus Christ:". He goes on to bless them saying that he desired God to multiply grace and peace to them, through the knowledge of God, and of Yeshua, our Lord. So, as believers, grace, and peace increase through the knowledge of God, and of course, His Son, Yeshua.

Then, Peter begins to speak of God's Divine power which God gave to all believers in things pertaining to life and godliness. Again, Peter mentions "through the knowledge of Him that has called us to glory and virtue". Knowledge of God, in Peter's eyes then, increases believers in grace and peace and leads believers into things pertaining to life and godliness.

These describe only a few aspects awaiting a believer who presses into God to understand and truly know God. How that knowledge manifests in a life of a believer, comes by a mutual choice between the believer and their pursuit of God, but the fact is, the more we desire to know God, not for what He can do, but for Who He is, the knowledge of Him clearly unfolds. To pursue God to those ends produces eternal values, among them, godliness here as we live our life before God upon the earth.

God, says Peter, has called us to glory and virtue. These attributes are not what the world clamours for, or even appreciates. These are things God desires to grow in His children, and the ends of a true knowledge of God. Peter knows this knowledge of God is something believers cannot obtain on their own, and thus he continues on to say, "whereby believers are given exceeding great and precious promises that by these you might partake of the divine nature".

That nature, of course, is the nature of God, which God expects to manifest in the lives of all those who know Him. That is a Second Covenant blessing given to believers in Messiah. All who enjoy the benefits of that covenant have made an escape, but what kind of an escape? Peter says, "having escaped the corruption that is in the world through lust." Why have believers escaped such corruption? Has God lifted them right out of the world in which they live?

Colossians 1:12-14
"Giving thanks unto the Father, which has made us ready to be partakers of the inheritance of the saints in light: Who has delivered us from the power of darkness, and has translated us into the kingdom of his dear Son: In whom we have redemption through his blood, even the forgiveness of sins:"

Physically, God does not remove the believer from the world in which they live, but He translates them spiritually from the power of darkness and places them, spiritually, in the kingdom of God's dear Son, which is Yeshua.

So, then, believers remain in the reality of this world in which they live, but what about their emotions or passions? Are these shut down, so they feel nothing? Of course not! Peter knows that the call of every believer is to live in the world, experience interaction with saved and unsaved alike. He knows their emotions and even their human passions exist, but their life must not operate from the lusts or passions of the world.

Peter knows, like the Apostle Paul who wrote Colossians 1:12-14, God translated us spiritually from under the power of darkness, and so we can manifest Godly responses, by the direction and power of the Holy Spirit, due to the Kingdom in which we now live, spiritually. To recap Peter's thoughts in a nutshell, he knows that those who live for the things of the world, live for things that satisfy their flesh, things that they think will make them happy!

Believers in Messiah, however, God calls to die to the things of the world but to awaken or come alive to the things of God, for therein lies *the opportunity* to escape the corruption in the world, through pursuing or yearning after the things of God. A believer's passions must experience a metamorphic change to thirst after God and to claim and express the passions of His heart as their own.

Such passions include desiring others to know God, seeing them saved from an eternal destiny away from God. It goes deeper too, for God desires each person who lives upon the earth to obtain their destiny, but that destiny we find in God alone. The ends of the pursuit of such destiny manifests in all virtue and godliness, as God sees it. Truly, the Christian life does not benefit by an escape from the world, but it is a lifestyle sought after, maintained, and expressed within the environment of the world in which we live. Such ends demonstrate to each believer, and to onlookers as well, the divine nature of God obtained through the precious promises.

Let us remember that God's divine nature, operative within, focuses the believer on longings for things neither sourced in the world nor found therein. No, a true believer's desire follows a different course of action as their pursuit opens them up for, and ends with, a transformation into the image of Yeshua. A believer's life must culminate in sincere responses like those of Yeshua, arising from a genuine heart of love, no matter the circumstances. This is how Yeshua responded. Such an end, certainly, only happens as the believers yield to the plans and purposes of God, which bring about God's desired destiny for His child.

In later verses, Peter goes on to say:

2 Peter 1:5-12
"And beside this, giving all diligence, add to your faith virtue; and to virtue knowledge; and to knowledge temperance; and to temperance patience; and to patience godliness; and to godliness brotherly kindness; and to brotherly kindness charity. For if these things be in you, and abound, they make you that you shall neither be barren nor unfruitful in the knowledge of our Lord Jesus Christ."

"But he that lacks these things is blind, and cannot see afar off, and has forgotten that he was purged from his old sins.

Wherefore the rather, brethren, give diligence to make your calling and election sure: for if you do these things, you shall never fall: For so an entrance shall be ministered unto you abundantly into the everlasting kingdom of our Lord and Saviour Jesus Christ. Wherefore I will not be negligent to put you always in remembrance of these things, though you know them, and be established in the present truth."

In this discourse, Peter gives a practical attitude to achieve such ends as genuinely responding like Messiah. He advises to focus, (give all diligence), to add to your faith in Messiah, "virtue", which in modern terms we might define as God's idea of moral excellence. To that moral excellence, one adds "knowledge". This alludes to a deep, intimate relationship with God. We see that by looking into the original text of the scripture:

In Greek, the word used for knowledge here is "γνῶσις":

Knowledge	Strong's # 1108	γνῶσις
	from 1097	gno'-sis
This root of this word refers to the intimate union in a marriage. It means to really "know" the other person.		

As Peter continues, he instructs believers to go past that intimate knowledge, adding "temperance", which is self-control, not allowing the "flesh" to rule over the house, *(meaning, the Temple of the Holy Spirit in which the believer dwells)*. After that, believers must add "patience", denoting a steadfast endurance to last the test of time. To that patience, one must add "godliness", that which reflects the holiness of God. That holiness comprises attitudes, words spoken and all actions towards God and man.

Continuing, in the formula of expressing God's Divine Nature, we add "brotherly kindness", treating fellow believers with carefulness, as we do family members. After all, their walk with God is just the same as ours: to crucify the flesh with its passions. Many scriptures speak of that fact. Below are just a few written by Paul, the Apostle:

Romans 8:13-14
"For if you live after the flesh, you shall die: but if you through the Spirit do mortify the deeds of the body, you shall live. For as many as are led by the Spirit of God, they are the sons of God."

2 Corinthians 10: 3
"For though we walk in the flesh, we do not war after the flesh:"

Galatians 5:16-17
"This I say then, Walk in the Spirit, and you shall not fulfil the lust of the flesh. For the flesh lusts against the Spirit, and the Spirit against the flesh: and these are contrary the one to the other: so that you cannot do the things that you would."

To understand that we are all in the same boat, all called to "die to the flesh", so to this brotherly kindness we add "love". Thus, this formula, once lived out, proves itself, not as barren nor as unfruitful, but rather, as we walk towards those ends of our faith, we indeed possess an intimate, working knowledge of our Lord, Yeshua Ha' Mashiach.

If, on the other hand, we lack these things, Peter tells us we are "blind". We cannot see ahead. Plainly put, we don't understand the ends where our faith wishes to take us. Such a one who is so blind forgets the washing away of theirs sins by the precious blood of the Lamb of God, for indeed, what a price He paid so we can attain the full ends of our faith.

Wherefore, says Peter, *or in modern words*, because of this, give diligence to make your calling and election sure. Do not let the ends of the faith escape your thoughts! Do not let it escape the true pursuit, the common ground that we have in this faith. Do not get your eyes on the wrong thing and pursue it! If you do, you'll end up with false hopes, shipwrecked. This, again the Apostle Paul states:

1 Timothy 1:18-20
"This charge I commit unto you, son Timothy, according to the prophecies which went before on you, that you by them might war a good warfare; Holding faith, and a good conscience; which some having put away concerning faith have made shipwreck; Of whom is Hymenaeus and Alexander; whom I have delivered unto ha satan, that they may learn not to blaspheme."

That is not the desired end, to put away the faith, and thus end up shipwrecked regarding the faith. Rather, believers should hold on to the sure foundation given to us. For if we endure to the end, following the formula Peter gave us, we won't fall, but rather receive entrance to the everlasting kingdom of our YeHoVaH, into eternity itself.

Therefore, Peter concludes in his discourse, he must be diligent to remind them of these things, to have them refer to the true ends of the faith, so they may know them and be firmly established in the present truth, in the world in which they live.

Here then, is Peter's formula for Christian living, backed up by the writings also of the Apostle, Paul:

PETER'S FORMULA FOR BELIEVERS

Pursue a true knowledge of God (which leads to a pursuit of virtue and godliness)

Obtaining God's promises that, by these, we partake of the divine nature, having escaped the corruption that is in the world through lust[29] (In other words, we thirst *after a relationship, which brings about a change in us.*

Add to the above

Virtue (moral excellence as God defines it)

Knowledge (a deep, intimate relationship with God)

Temperance, (the Spirit rules the flesh)

Patience (steadfast endurance to stand the test of time)

Godliness, (character which reflects the holiness of God)

Brotherly Kindness (Remembering God calls us to the same ends, the crucified life.)

RESULTS

Live as God designed, employing His formula for living, we will see the ultimate destiny of God for our lives including the awesome partaking of God's Divine nature, expressing it daily, with words and deeds. We

---

[29] *2 Peter 1:4 Whereby are given unto us exceeding great and precious promises: that by these ye might be partakers of the divine nature, having escaped the corruption that is in the world through lust.*

will then make our calling and election sure, knowing the present truth to which we are called, and as we follow that truth, enduring until the end, we enter eternity, into God's Kingdom receiving great rewards.

Peter's message might easily find its understanding in a parable spoken by Yeshua:

John 12: 24-26
"Truly, truly, I say unto you, Except a corn of wheat fall into the ground and die, it abides alone: but if it die, it brings forth much fruit. He that loves his life shall lose it; and he that hates his life in this world shall keep it unto life eternal. If any man serves me, let him follow me; and where I am, there shall also my servant be: if any man serve me, him will my Father honour."

A corn of wheat planted into the ground dies. From that death comes forth new life. That life brings forth fruit, and within that fruit come more seeds to sow and see the corn multiply. Such a farmer's increases bring him great joy and as he continues to sow the seed into the ground, his seed wealth increases. Instead, if he kept the one seed on the shelf, at the end, he has but one seed.

In comparing this parable to the life of a believer, we see that holding on to our life, living it our way, is the same thing as letting a seed sit on a shelf, not planted.

All you have at the end is the seed. This life is unfruitful in God's eyes. It is far better to live our lives, not looking for the fulfillment of what we desire in ourselves, but rather deny such, and die to the things that offend God.

Our life, here in the flesh, must be like the corn of wheat sown into the ground. We experience "death" to the temporal desires of the flesh; we live the crucified life. In doing so, we spring forth in a new budding life, expressing the image of Yeshua. This makes a life fruitful in the eyes of God. This is truly living as a servant to God and the end of such a life will culminate in a life with Yeshua for all eternity.

To these ends we must live our faith, and in doing so, as we chose to live in a similar manner to that grain of wheat placed in the ground to die, we see our God and His power displayed in us, clearly visible by the dynamic changes, affected by the Holy Spirit in and through us. Thus, we do see God as mighty in our midst. This then is a comparable experience with God, which the early, first century church knew:

Zephaniah 3: 17-18
"YeHoVaH your God in the midst of you [is] mighty; he will save, he will rejoice over you with joy; he will rest in his love, he will joy over you with singing. I will gather them that

are sorrowful for the solemn assembly, who are of you, to whom the reproach of it was a burden."

Somehow in today's Christendom, many think God's only way of showing His might in our midst, is to do some miracle for us to see. Sadly, believers only look for an outside performance of the power of God to recognize God in our midst. Some fail to see beyond that outer witness, sometimes overlooking God's transforming power *within a believer*. While believers can and should rejoice when a miraculous healing manifests in a person's body, let us remember to look to other aspects of God's presence in our midst and rejoice when a life of a drug addict, alcoholic or prostitute, mightily changes by the power of God! This, too, shows God in our midst as mighty.

While we desire to see bodies healed, let us also desire to see manifestations of a truly transformed life. If our brother or sister faces a trial, let us pray for God's help in their time of need. Let us not abandon them, but if we can, let us walk with them until they reach the other side of their trial. As we do, let us not forget the transforming power of God to act within that person, or within us.

Let us learn to rejoice at the character changes that God implants within the believers through their trial. Let us learn to joy in the faith, suffering, if need be, not for doing evil, but rather for doing good. This is an early, first century church mindset as we see it displayed in the Book of Acts, after the author records the severe beating of the disciples by the officials of Judaism:

Acts 5:41
"And they departed from the presence of the council, rejoicing that they were counted worthy to suffer shame for his name."

Here, the Jewish leaders in the city of Jerusalem beat the disciples to stop them speaking in the Name of Yeshua. It did not work! The attitudes, expressed by the apostles, were not what the authorities expected. They anticipated them to cease their activities, not to count themselves worthy to suffer!

1 Peter 4:15-19
"But let none of you suffer as a murderer, or as a thief, or as an evildoer, or as a busybody in other men's matters. Yet if any man suffer as a Christian, let him not be ashamed; but let him glorify God on this behalf. For the time is come that judgment must begin at the house of God: and if it first begin at us, what shall the end be of them that obey not the gospel of God? And if the righteous scarcely be saved, where shall the ungodly and the sinner appear? Wherefore let them that suffer according to the will of God commit the keeping of their souls to him in well doing, as unto a faithful Creator."

Peter, one of the apostles beaten by the Jews, *(as we read in our earlier scripture from the book of Acts),* advises his listeners not to suffer shame when persecuted, but rather glorify God. He sees the end of such as a good thing and advises the sufferer to commit their souls to God, in well doing. This attitude is certainly not one we hear today in our churches but is perhaps one we should strongly consider.

CHAPTER'S SUMMARY
In this chapter, we approached the subject of recognizing God's might as it is displayed in us. This might of God is seen in believers as we embrace the crucified life, pursuing the things of God, which include a changed life, embracing, experiencing, and expressing the Divine Nature of God. We looked at Peter's formula for living the Christian life. We saw that to follow that formula we need the Godkind of faith. The end of such faith is that, as we die and allow God to fulfill His purpose in life, we receive our destiny in Him, and show Him as mighty in our midst.

How awesome to think of His might in this fashion! We concluded with two scriptures that spoke of trials and sufferings. One scripture spoke of Peter, and some other disciples, beaten for their faith, in an effort by the Jews to stop them preaching the resurrection, and a second scripture giving advice from Peter, not to suffer shame if they suffer for their faith. Let's learn to grasp the God kind of faith, determined to live that faith until the end, no matter the cost.

As we think about God's might in our midst, let us pursue Him to see it manifested in our changed character

SECTION 2

Consider God's Ways

"Consider Him that endured such contradiction of sinners against himself, lest you be wearied and faint in your minds."
Hebrews 12:3

WHEN ESTABLISHING HIS PLANS

6

"O the depth of the riches both of the wisdom and knowledge of God! how unsearchable are his judgments, and his ways past finding out! For who has known the mind of YeHoVaH? or who has been his counsellor? Or who has first given to him, and it shall be recompensed unto him again? For of him, and through him, and to him, are all things: to whom be glory for ever. Amen."

Romans 11:33-36

*O*UR OPENING SCRIPTURE originates from the Apostle Paul's letter to believers at Rome. Chapter 11 includes this wonderful dissertation from the Apostle Paul regarding God's chosen nation, Israel, in the timeframe immediately *after the cross* of Yeshua. As the chapter opens, in verse 1, Paul asks an important question of the recipients of his letter: *"Has God cast off His people, the Jews?"*

Certainly, this was a good question, for in those days of the early, first century church, some Jews received the gospel message proclaiming Yeshua as Messiah, but in comparison to the number of Gentiles embracing the Messiah, Jewish numbers were few. If one studied the facts in front of them, it was easy to see that the bulk of Judaism rejected Yeshua as the Messiah, and in fact, many of them responded in anger. That anger and their objections to those who followed Yeshua as Messiah, Paul well understood. Prior to his conversion, he held the same viewpoint and was one who ardently undertook to cease and imprison the believers following Yeshua as Messiah. Since Israel, for the most part, did not react well to the gospel message, those who did receive it wondered what would happen to Israel. Would God cast them off?

God forbid was Paul's answer. Then, Paul begins to explain God's viewpoint regarding Israel. God, says Paul, always has a faithful remnant of His people. While Paul did not lay out his scriptural evidence for his viewpoint in the book of Romans, his reference to a remnant originates in the book of Kings, sourced from the life of the prophet, Elijah. Elijah was God's prophet to Northern Israel, centuries before Paul. Fearing for his life, Elijah had run and hid in a cave. God brings Elijah out of the cave and asks him this question: "What are you doing here, Elijah?"[30] Elijah responds bravely, with these words:

1 Kings 19:14
"And he said, I have been very jealous for YeHoVaH God of hosts: because the children of Israel have forsaken your covenant, thrown down your altars, and slain your prophets with the sword; and I, even I only, am left; and they seek my life, to take it away."

Elijah's focus on the overwhelming sin he saw in God's people at that time, had left him in great discouragement. His human conclusion of the situation, however, was not accurate because Elijah did not have all the facts. To Elijah, he was the only faithful servant of God left alive and soon his life would be gone, if those who wanted him dead actually got hold of him.

Elijah exclaims, from a deeply broken heart, "Who then would remain to serve YeHoVaH?" God's response to Elijah was to open his eyes to see the situation more accurately:

---

[30] 1 Kings 19:13

1 Kings 19: 18
"Yet I have left me seven thousand in Israel, all the knees which have not bowed unto Baal, and every mouth which has not kissed him."

God, as always, knew the bigger picture, the one, due to circumstances, Elijah failed to grasp. Understanding this greater picture, the view God shared with Elijah, is extremely important. The first lesson is rather obvious. God had seven thousand left who had not bowed the knee to Baal, nor kissed him. The other lesson, one to which we need pay close attention, is that Elijah's perspective was linked only to his human wisdom. God showed Elijah a lesson from which, anyone, in any generation, could benefit: no matter the situation, apart from a release of God's wisdom, humankind only sees what's in front of him.

We human beings, no matter how faithfully we may serve YeHoVaH, will neither see, nor comprehend, the bigger picture in any situation *unless* God gives us His understanding in the matter. Unfortunately, we will see things with our own eyes, our own wisdom and usually handle things with our own resolve. It is far better to look at things God's way. In this case, what Elijah could not see was that he was not alone in serving God. Seven thousand more faithful servants stood firm as a remnant in that moment of time, and as Paul states, God always has a remnant.

Returning now to the Apostle Paul and his dissertation in Romans Chapter 11, he relates to the bigger picture to those in Rome: "God has not cast off His people!" Even at the time of this writing of the book to the Romans, Paul knew God had a remnant, just like in the days of Elijah. In fact, Paul, himself, was part of that remnant, as he and some other Jews of his day, opened their heart to receive Yeshua as the Messiah and picked up the torch to carry His message throughout the world at that time.

To help those at Rome look past what their human eyes saw and what their minds might conclude, Paul explains that the Jews received a spirit of slumber, with eyes darkened, that they should not see and ears that they would not hear, and backs bowed down always. Yet, even in that, God had a purpose:

Romans 11:11-12
"I say then, Have they stumbled that they should fall? God forbid: but rather through their fall salvation is come unto the Gentiles, for to provoke them to jealousy. Now if the fall of them be the riches of the world, and the diminishing of them the riches of the Gentiles; how much more their fulness?"

God's plan could never include a forsaking of His people, the Jews. God's greater plan, the bigger picture, shows rather that their rejection of Yeshua as the Messiah opened wide a door to the Gentiles. That very action provoked the Jews to jealousy. Paul goes on to say, consider "how the fall of them" (in reference to their rejection of the Messiah) brings so great a salvation to the Gentiles. Later, Paul reassures believers, that the Jews will receive Yeshua as their Messiah.

A comparison follows, in continuing verses in Chapter 11, as Paul illustrates the people of Israel living under that First Covenant, as natural branches of the olive tree, which presently were cut off for their disbelief.

Romans 11:19-26
"You will say then, The branches were broken off, that I might be grafted in. Well; because of unbelief they were broken off, and you stand by faith. Be not high-minded, but fear: For if God spared not the natural branches, [take heed] lest he also spare not you. Behold therefore the goodness and severity of God: on them which fell, severity; but toward you, goodness, if you continue in [his] goodness: otherwise you also shall be cut off. And they also, if they abide not still in unbelief, shall be grafted in: for God is able to graft them in again. For if you were cut out of the olive tree which is wild by nature, and were grafted contrary to nature into a good olive tree: how much more shall these, which be the natural [branches], be grafted into their own olive tree?"

Gentiles were branches grafted in, but when God grafts back in the natural branches, how much will those branches flourish!

Paul then states:

Romans 11: 25-36
"For I would not, brethren, that you should be ignorant of this mystery, lest you should be wise in your own conceits; that blindness in part is happened to Israel, until the fulness of the Gentiles be come in. And so all Israel shall be saved: as it is written, There shall come out of Sion the Deliverer, and shall turn away ungodliness from Jacob: For this is my covenant unto them, when I shall take away their sins. As concerning the gospel, they are enemies for your sakes: but as touching the election, they are beloved for the fathers' sakes. For the gifts and calling of God are without repentance. For as you in times past have not believed God, yet have now obtained mercy through their unbelief: Even so have these also now not believed, that through your mercy they also may obtain mercy. For God has concluded them all in unbelief, that he might have mercy upon all."

Again, the Apostle Paul stresses the blindness which happened to Israel and how it benefits the Gentiles. Once the fullness of the Gentiles comes, then it is time for Israel again. Paul makes it very clear that the gifts and calling of God are without repentance, meaning neither turned back nor removed. One more time, Paul mentions that God concluded them all in unbelief, that God might have mercy upon all people. Then comes this wonderful verse:

Romans 11:33-36
"O the depth of the riches both of the wisdom and knowledge of God! how unsearchable are his judgments, and his ways past finding out! For who has known the mind of YeHoVaH? or who has been his counsellor? Or who has first given to him, and it shall be recompensed unto him again? For of him, and through him, and to him, are all things: to whom be glory for ever. Amen."

Paul declares that God's wisdom and knowledge are unfathomable in their depth. Neither God's Ways, nor judgments are ever completely searched out by man.

No man can possess greater knowledge than God and certainly no man can advise God, either. Paul continues with his questions: Who first gave to God, and in return, God owes them something in return? No one, Paul says, for it is all about God! All things are for God, through Him and to Him. Thus, to God be the glory, forever and ever.

In other words, children of God at Rome and for all of time, remember this: it is all about God and not about man. God was, and is, and always will be the superior one to Whom we bow! Surely God's Ways are deep, the sum of them beyond our understanding; "God's ways are past finding out", meaning believers cannot know that sum total of His ways, however, we can know some of those ways.

Looking back over the earlier verses in Romans 11, to keep things in context, we see Paul's explanation of one avenue of God's wisdom and knowledge. Through this chapter we realize that yes, God called the Jews unto Himself to serve Him and be a light to all nations, but their blindness prevented the entirety of them from receiving Yeshua as their long-awaited Messiah. That didn't mean God cast them off, washing His hands of them, or turning His back on them and walking away. No way! Rather, Israel reacted to the Messiah, Yeshua, *in a manner exactly as God knew they would act*. Their response opened a marvellous door for the Gentile's salvation.

Once the fullness of the Gentiles comes in, then the partial lifting of their blindness changes to a total removal of that blindness from the eyes of the Jews. How inclusive of all mankind is God's plan? Who could have ever thought of it? Who could ever have given God advise on that plan or how to accomplish the salvation of the world? Absolutely no human being! It was unquestionably too marvellous, yes, past finding out!

As we read this passage of the Apostle in Romans, we actually see one of God's ways opened up before our eyes. It shows us that His wisdom, His knowledge, His judgments, which are so far above the head of mankind, are never completely grasped until the time of its revelation. What does that tell us about God?

There are many lessons here, but first, let's look at this one important fact:

> *God desires man to recognize that they have a desperate need of Him, and from such, call out to Him and from there, learn to walk with Him.*

Let's think about this as we review some people of faith whose lives bear witness to that truth.

ABRAHAM
To Abraham, a man involved in idolatry, the God of glory appeared:

Joshua 24:2
"And Joshua said unto all the people, Thus says YeHoVaH God of Israel, Your fathers dwelt on the other side of the flood in old time, [even] Terah, the father of Abraham, and the father of Nachor: and they served other gods."

Acts 7:2
"And he said, Men, brethren, and fathers, hearken; The God of glory appeared unto our father Abraham, when he was in Mesopotamia, before he dwelt in Charran,"

God led him, step by step, calling him out of the land where he was born. He showed Abraham salvation, promising also to give this man, a son. Abraham's wife, Sarah, was barren, but the promise of a son, Abraham believed. Somehow God would keep His Word. As Sarah and Abraham thought about this promise, they stayed within the normal parameters of what is known to man. They concluded that if Sarah could not bear a child, then God must have another plan. Surely, the custom of their day was the answer. God would give Abraham a son through Sarah's maid servant, Hagar. This is how God will do it? So, Sarah gives her handmaiden to Abraham, and later, through Abraham and Hagar comes forth a son named Ishmael. This son, to their surprise, was not the son God promised. God had a different plan.

It was not until Abraham was 100 years old and Sarah 90 years old, well past childbearing years of that generation, that God alone brought His promise to fruition. God visited them, after which Sarah conceived a child by Abraham. No hand of man, no custom of their day, no human intervention whatsoever could take responsibility for that birth. It was God, and God alone, Who gave them their son. In Abraham, just as God promised, and through Sarah came a seed from whom all the nations of the world will be blessed.

Genesis 18: 18
"Seeing that Abraham shall surely become a great and mighty nation, and all the nations of the earth shall be blessed in him?"

In this situation, man's wisdom, man's knowledge and understanding failed entirely to grasp what God decided. God's promised son lay far beyond the possibilities of man to obtain on their own. Pursuing that course meant futility. God's ways are higher than those of man, even higher than the natural order of things that God created in the universe. Abraham and Sarah looked higher and entered the realm of faith in order to obtain their promise:

Hebrews 11:8-12
"By faith Abraham, when he was called to go out into a place which he should after receive for an inheritance, obeyed; and he went out, not knowing where he went. By faith he sojourned in the land of promise, as in a strange country, dwelling in tabernacles with Isaac and Jacob, the heirs with him of the same promise: For he looked for a city which has foundations, whose builder and maker is God. Through faith also Sara herself received strength to conceive seed, and

was delivered of a child when she was past age, because she judged him faithful who had promised. Therefore, sprang there even of one, and him as good as dead, so many as the stars of the sky in multitude, and as the sand which is by the sea shore innumerable."

Faith in God, to the human thought processes, seems most unnatural. Yet, this is the wisdom God set in place, as a principle in our universe:

1 Corinthians 1: 27
"But God has chosen the foolish things of the world to confound the wise; and God has chosen the weak things of the world to confound the things which are mighty;"

Believers, of all ages, must learn to look to God and trust Him as did Abraham, even when all the logical facts in front of you point out great impossibilities. Yet, faith and its principle, embraced by man, is one of God's ways as He deals with mankind!

DAVID

King David lived at a time when the kingdom of Israel held very little of the promised land that God assigned to them to obtain and maintain. By the time King David arrived on the scene, Joshua, a powerful leader over Israel after Moses, had died.

Throughout the generations that followed these children of Israel, other leaders called judges rose to lead Israel, yet still generations later, Israel suffered oppression from other nations in the land, nations God wanted them to remove but neither their faith nor their forces could dislodge. In looking for a solution, the people demanded a king, so they, like other nations, would have a powerful, human leader. Surely that was their answer! Reluctantly, God gave them Saul.

King Saul failed miserably in his task as king for this man neither understood God, nor God's Ways. Not too long into Saul's reign, we find God rejects Saul as King. Saul remained physically in the position as King, but God withdrew His anointing from Saul and placed it on another, more worthy. This anointing, however, was done in private, for fear that Saul would discover his replacement and undertake to remove him.

Samuel the prophet, following God's lead, secretly anoints a young boy named David. Later, as David arrives publicly on the scene, he does so at a time when both Saul and his army faced a giant named Goliath. Saul promised great rewards if only someone would arise and remove this giant. To the King and the soldiers, the person to accept the challenge must be strong and mighty, well trained in the art of war. He must certainly possess great courage and strength to remove that daunting giant in full armour, standing before them grasping his gigantic sword. However, no trained soldier in Saul's army came forward. Instead, fear of the giant Goliath, immobilized Israel's army.

Then, this young boy named David, the one God had secretly anointed as King, arrives upon the scene. He possesses no armour, no sword, no helmet, and no experience in battle, yet he bravely faces the giant in the name of YeHoVaH of Hosts.

1 Samuel 17: 45-47
"Then said David to the Philistine, You come to me with a sword, and with a spear, and with a shield: but I come to you in the name of YeHoVaH of hosts, the God of the armies of Israel, whom you have defied. This day will YeHoVaH deliver you into my hand; and I will smite you, and take your head from you; and I will give the carcases of the host of the Philistines this day unto the fowls of the air, and to the wild beasts of the earth; that all the earth may know that there is a God in Israel. And all this assembly shall know that YeHoVaH saves not with sword and spear: for the battle is YeHoVaH'S, and he will give you into our hands."

This challenge, too fearful for seasoned warriors to face, God met through this young boy David, who not only had great faith, but also loved God with all his heart. David, even though very young,[31] realized that

---

[31] David was probably around the age of 14

this battle was not his own, nor the soldiers in Saul's armies. He saw it as defiance against God and His armies; therefore, this was God's battle!

David boldly declared that God, by His hand, would remove the giant Goliath and the host of the Philistines. Using neither sword, nor spear, but only a sling shot and a stone, David faces Goliath. Trusting God, David throws the stone from the sling shot and fells Goliath. He then takes Goliath's own sword and removes the giant's head.

The armies of Israel, seeing the giant defeated by a young body, regained their courage, and chased the Philistines out of the territory they formerly possessed, thus advancing Israel's territories, in line with what God gave them.

In that unique situation, on that day, when King Saul and his armies were paralyzed with fear, God introduced a young boy who knew the ways of God, a young boy who walked by faith, and trusted God. As we reflect upon this young boy's life, and his later reign as King of Israel, we see David possessed a heart that longed after God. Of this, the New Testament reminds us:

Acts 13:22
"And when he had removed him32, he raised up unto them David to be their king; to whom also he gave testimony, and said, I have found David the son of Jesse, a man after my own heart, which shall fulfil all my will."

WHAT DOES ALL THIS MEAN?

As we look at Abraham's situation and that situation which King David faced as a boy, we find a reinforcement of the fact that God desires faith in His people[33]. Yet, there is another lesson here, perhaps a little less obvious. It is that God loves a situation that is too big for man.

Our Bible is full of such circumstances where some person is way out there in his inability to do something. Insurmountable odds prevail against them, and just when they thought their goose was cooked, just when it looked like devastation would have its way, someone puts their faith in God. God then shows up with a mighty hand and impacts everything around, resolving the situation and showing Himself as strong. In fact, we hear that God ardently looks for such places to show Himself strong:

---

[32] Referring to King Saul
[33] *Hebrews 10:38 Now the just shall live by faith: but if any man draw back, my soul shall have no pleasure in him.*

Chapter 6 — When Establishing His Plans

2 Chronicles 16:9
"For the eyes of YeHoVaH run to and fro throughout the whole earth, to show himself strong in the behalf of them whose heart is perfect toward him. Herein you have done foolishly: therefore from henceforth you shall have wars."

In this situation, King Asa of Judah foolishly looked to another source, other than God, for his deliverance from the enemies threatening his life, and the lives of all Judah. King Asa, however, thought the King of Syria was his answer and thus, he puts his plans in place. After those plans were solidified, God sends the seer Hanani to speak to King Asa. Hanani plainly tells the king that God's eyes run everywhere throughout the earth looking for a place to show Himself as strong, on behalf of those whose hearts trust God, or look to Him for the needed answer.

In modern lingo, the seer tells the king, "you missed it". Right in front of King Asa was a marvellous opportunity. Certainly, it frightened him; certainly, it overwhelmed him and certainly, it needed an immediate response. If he only had given that situation to YeHoVaH for God's intended solution, he would have done well, for God looks for just the sort of situation facing King Asa. "You missed it, King Asa, because you put your trust in man and not in God".

God desires that we trust Him. In the case of King Asa in 2 Chronicles, God's plan, if asked for help, may well have included sending an army to help the king, but not necessarily! God has been known throughout scripture to have some very creative plans. He has sent enemies back for various reasons; some armies have turned and fought amongst themselves and thus God's people enjoyed deliverance. God's plans are unlimited in scope, and His reach, far beyond man's understanding. It is possible that God might use a person, a king, an army, or perhaps choose another way, but whatever the solution, this King Asa did not receive it. Why? Because he trusted in man, in his own solution, in his own wisdom, his own knowledge, his own political maneuverings of his day, rather than trust in the solutions of God.

CHAPTER'S SUMMARY
We saw, in this chapter, the early church in Rome trying to gain a full understanding of Israel's destiny, one they found perplexing. At that time, current events regarding Israel disturbed them. With more Gentiles coming to Messiah all the time, and the Jews resisting the idea of Yeshua as the Messiah, what was ever going to happen to Israel?

Paul explains that it is impossible for mankind to really know the mind of YeHoVaH unless God opens their mind to Divine revelation. Paul, through his knowledge of scripture and his calling and relationship with YeHoVaH, received such from YeHoVaH. So, he revealed to the recipients of his letter, God's inclusive plan for all nations, now and in the future, as all Israel receives the Messiah.

As we read the pages in this chapter, we quickly looked at Abraham, Sarah, and King David to see circumstances beyond the help of man. Surely, we rejoiced to see how God revived Abraham who then implanted a seed within the womb of his 90-year-old wife, a woman long past her childbearing years.

How awesome, too, was the battle where a young boy named David faces Goliath, a giant that Israel's army refused to fight. David, small in stature, but mighty in faith, identifies the battle as YeHoVaH's and through this incident, Israel sees the removal of a wall of fear and advances forward to their God-given destiny.

We ended that section with a look at a foolish King, Asa, who made his own decision to solve his dilemma, and in doing so, missed his opportunity to show God as strong, stronger than the attacking enemy forces. From this we can conclude that, on the surface, when we see situations in front of us, which may seem challenging even overwhelming, God prefers we discover a resolution by not using our own wisdom and knowledge, but rather pursuing Him for His.

We see God's wisdom as we study the scriptures and the principles therein. In reading and learning these, in developing a deep relationship with Him, as those scriptures outline, we will absolutely find God's answers. We might not instantly know this, nor how God will move in any situation; nor how He will resolve it either, but from scripture's examples and lessons, we can determine not to handle it on our own, apart from God's help. God establishes His Plan for a greater benefit than we might understand.

Let's remember, God is greater than any situation His children shall ever face. We must learn to give everything over to Him, big and small, and let Him prove Himself strong, standing with His children to get them through in victory to the other side! Indeed, our God loves a challenge! He is not asleep in our generation, nor in any other.

YeHoVaH is the same God today as He was in Bible days. He is the same God that parted the Red Sea; the same God that gave manna in the desert; the same God that breathed into a virgin's womb to bring forth to all mankind, a Saviour that saves to the uttermost all those who draw near unto Him! God has not changed! He is very much alive and wants us to know His Ways. One of those ways is that God loves a place, and looks for situations, where He can show Himself strong.

Let's learn to release every challenge in our life to YeHoVaH as a place to show Himself as strong! Let us wait on Him to reveal to us His mind in this matter!

God holds greater plans for us than we can possibly think. Let's learn to think His Way.

WHEN RELEASING HIS REWARDS

7

"Oh how great is your goodness, which you have laid up for them that fear you, which you have brought for them that trust in you before the sons of men! You shall hide them in the secret of your presence from the pride of man: you shall keep them secretly in a pavilion from the strife of tongues.
Psalm 31:19-20

*I**N THE SCRIPTURE* passage above, King David looked to God for deliverance. As Psalm 31 opens, King David pleads with God for a speedy deliverance. He rehearses God's goodness to him, and gently speaks to God of the oppression of those who hate David, and all for which he stands. Before we hear King David declare God's goodness in this Psalm, we hear some of his heart's cry:

Psalm 31:11-13
"I was a reproach among all my enemies, but especially among my neighbours, and a fear to my acquaintance: they that did see me without fled from me. I am forgotten as a dead man out of mind: I am like a broken vessel. For I have heard the slander of many: fear was on every side: while they took counsel together against me, they devised to take away my life."

In these verses, we see David bearing his soul to YeHoVaH, clearly describing the pain he experienced. Even so, King David makes a declaration of his trust in God:

Psalm 31:14-18
"But I trusted in you, YeHoVaH: I said, You are my God. My times are in your hand: deliver me from the hand of my enemies, and from them that persecute me. Make your face to shine upon your servant: save me for your mercies' sake. Let me not be ashamed, YeHoVaH; for I have called upon you: let the wicked be ashamed and let them be silent in the grave. Let the lying lips be put to silence, which speak grievous things proudly and contemptuously against the righteous."

Along with a declaration of David's trust, we hear David's clear understanding that his life is in God's Hand. Then, he returns to plead for deliverance from those who persecute him. He continues to ask God to shine His face upon David and save him, not because he deserves it, rather because of the sake of God's mercy. He does not wish shame to be his end here but rather asks YeHoVaH for the shame of the wicked, whose accusing words would then be silent in the grave. Yes, lying lips would be silent as they speak grievous things with pride and contention against the righteous. Then King David declares:

Psalm 31: 19-24
"Oh how great is your goodness, which you have laid up for them that fear you, which you have brought for them that trust in you before the sons of men! You shall hide them in the secret of your presence from the pride of man: you shall keep them secretly in a pavilion from the strife of tongues. Blessed be YeHoVaH: for he has showed me his marvellous kindness in a strong city. For I said in my haste, I am cut off from before your eyes: nevertheless you heard the voice of my supplications when I cried unto you. O love YeHoVaH, all ye his saints: for YeHoVaH preserves the faithful and plentifully rewards the proud doer. Be of good courage, and he shall strengthen your heart, all you that hope in YeHoVaH."

"Oh, how great is thy goodness?" says King David. Indeed, God has laid up good things for those who love Him, to those who trust in God as their primary source of deliverance, rather than omitting that trust and putting it elsewhere.

To those, God hides in the secret place of His presence. In that secret place one will never find the pride of man, nor the strife of their tongues. Even though King David felt that he was cut off from God, yet God heard his voice when David cried out to him with his supplications. Then David tells those set apart for God's kingdom, God's saints, YeHoVaH preserves the faithful and rewards the proud doer. Therefore, cheer up when you are downhearted, David says, for God shall strengthen in heart all those that hope in YeHoVaH.

To those who experience the love and mercy of the God, such as King David, they easily attest to God's goodness. Knowing the situations where life and its choices led them, they received deliverance as they called upon God. These can now look back and appreciate God's goodness and open their mouths to attest to God's His mercy and goodness. Hopefully their testimony will speak to others. While that does happen, it is often the case where others hear of such things and refuse to receive what they've heard. Some even go so far as to mock the testimony or distain

God's chosen leaders, those God would call His Servants. Such was King David's experience as many lashed out with their words against his legitimate kingship and rule over God's people. Yet, King David kept his eyes upon YeHoVaH. He understood something they did not grasp: *the many ways of God.*

Many, who don't understand such ways, may seek God for understanding, but there are those who decide to mock the things of God, call them nonsense, even rubbish. These people are blind to God's realities, realities that cannot be seen by human eyes, but rather the eyes of faith. All through the Bible we hear of such things, and even in the days when Yeshua walked the earth, it was so. Yeshua's role, for example, as a suffering Messiah, was not perceived, even though the scriptures foretold it:

Isaiah 53:1-12
"Who has believed our report? and to whom is the arm of YeHoVaH revealed? For he shall grow up before him as a tender plant, and as a root out of a dry ground: he has no form nor comeliness; and when we shall see him, [there is] no beauty that we should desire him. He is despised and rejected of men; a man of sorrows and acquainted with grief: and we hid as it were [our] faces from him; he was despised, and we esteemed him not."

"Surely, he hath borne our griefs, and carried our sorrows: yet we did esteem him stricken, smitten of God, and afflicted. But he [was] wounded for our transgressions, [he was] bruised for our iniquities: the chastisement of our peace [was] upon him; and with his stripes we are healed. All we like sheep have gone astray; we have turned everyone to his own way; and YeHoVaH hath laid on him the iniquity of us all."

"He was oppressed, and he was afflicted, yet he opened not his mouth: he is brought as a lamb to the slaughter, and as a sheep before her shearers is dumb, so he opened not his mouth. He was taken from prison and from judgment: and who shall declare his generation? for he was cut off out of the land of the living: for the transgression of my people was he stricken. And he made his grave with the wicked, and with the rich in his death; because he had done no violence, neither [was any] deceit in his mouth."

"Yet it pleased YeHoVaH to bruise him; he put [him] to grief: when you shall make his soul an offering for sin, he shall see [his] seed, he shall prolong [his] days, and the pleasure of YeHoVaH shall prosper in his hand. 11 He shall see of the travail of his soul [and] shall be satisfied: by his knowledge shall my righteous servant justify many; for he shall bear their iniquities. Therefore will I divide him [a portion] with the great, and he shall divide the spoil with the strong; because he has poured out his soul unto death: and *he was numbered with the transgressors; and he bore the sin of many and made intercession for the transgressors."*

Once Messiah suffered, died, and lay in the tomb three days, God rose Him up. He, some time later, breathed upon His Disciples and opened their minds to the scriptures. Then they clearly saw the plan of God set in place, a suffering Messiah. Isaiah clearly declared the Messiah as despised and rejected, but God's people thought only of Israel's acceptance of their Messiah.

While the scriptures declared that Messiah would know grief with the scriptures about the Messiah suffering did not connect with their thinking[34]. Instead, they looked at His life and saw the grief as God's punishment for the man. To them, this man was of no importance! He was rather one ill-favoured of God.

Isaiah, however, prophesied that the Messiah would bear our griefs and carry our sorrows. He went on to say that others would perceive Him as punished by God's hand and afflicted by Him. Yet, in reality, He was wounded for our transgressions, bruised for our iniquities; and the chastisement of our peace [was] upon him; and with His flesh torn by the Roman whip, the marks of the whip scripture call "His stripes," and

---

[34] That revelation about the Messiah, Yeshua's disciples received after the resurrection.

as the Apostle Peter tells us, "By His stripes we were healed."[35]

Furthermore, Isaiah goes on to say that everyone is like a sheep that has wandered away. Each one has made his own choice, gone his own way, but YeHoVaH laid all humanity's iniquity upon Him. This Messiah knew oppression, knew affliction, but He never complained or said a word in His own defence. Isaiah describes Him as a sheep led to the slaughter. He was taken to a prison house, to judgment, where the sentence assigned to Him was death. As scripture says, "He was cut Him off from the land of the living". Why? Isaiah tells us, "for the transgression of my people it was so". This man was buried with the wicked and the rich in his death because he was innocent. No violence or deceit was found in his mouth.

This all happened because God was pleased to bruise Him, to put Him to grief, making his soul an offering for sin. Yet, Isaiah says, His seed shall be seen by Him, His days shall be prolonged, and He will see the travail of his soul and be satisfied. By His knowledge, says Isaiah, God's righteous suffering servant, would justify many for He will bear their iniquities.

---

[35] *1 Peter 2:24*

Due to that sacrifice, God allotted Him a portion with great men. He shall divide the spoil with the other strong victors of battle, because He poured out his soul unto death, even numbered with the transgressors. He bore the sin of many and made intercession for the transgressors, says Isaiah.

This entire chapter in Isaiah is a very clear description of a suffering Messiah, who bore the sins of the world, yet was rejected by His own. God's plan for the Messiah to bear the sins of the world, and to suffer rejection by His own people, although prophesied a long time before, was hidden from the eyes of God's people, until the day God allowed the prophecy to come to fruition and later, opened blinded eyes to perceive the truth.

From this lesson, believers can realize that God's plans hold a depth that no one knows and may well go against thought processes which some of God's people perceive, *measuring the blessings of God's in terms of earthly value.*

In our day, due to some rather strange teachings which advocate prosperity as God's measuring stick of blessing, many believers, perhaps unconsciously, learn to measure God's blessings by visual expressions of financial status or by looking at the outward show of some material benefit to indicate blessings. Believers may see one to whom God gives a large home with well furnished appointments, situated on a large lot in a secluded neighbourhood, and thus perceive that person as one truly blessed of God.

On the other hand, believers may look at a lonely widow, barely getting by financially; and they may perceive she is somewhat less blessed by God. In God's eyes, it is possible that one might be more blessed than the other, but the physical evidence shown on the outside may not give the proper clue as to which one is more blessed by God.

Has any person in the Bible ever been able to judge the heart of another, identifying their service to God by an outward show of God's blessings? In considering an answer to that question, we come across a man who lived in the time of David, before he was crowned king. This man had great wealth, as easily seen by those who assessed him, but this man did not understand God, nor God's blessings and its purpose, nor the times and season wherein the man lived.

1 Samuel 25:2-3
"And there was a man in Maon, whose possessions were in Carmel; and the man was very great, and he had three thousand sheep, and a thousand goats: and he was shearing his sheep in Carmel. Now the name of the man was Nabal; and the name of his wife Abigail: and she was a woman of

good understanding, and of a beautiful countenance: but the man was rude mannered and evil in his doings; and he was of the house of Caleb."

Nabal was a very rich man, and amongst his treasures was the blessing of a beautiful and virtuous wife. This man, unfortunately, decided not to share so much as a little food for David and his men. David, at that time, although anointed by God as King, did not yet rule on the throne but, due to circumstances, was running from Saul, who, because of God's anointing upon David, tried to kill him.

At the time this event took place, David, a renegade in the eyes of many, camped near the fields of Nabal and David, being the man of integrity that he was, watched over Nabal's sheep, keeping them from harm. Then, at a point when David and his men hungered, and who were able to simply take what they needed, acted with upright behaviour and sent to ask Nabal for food. Nabal promptly refused.

Abigail, the man's wife, heard of this event and immediately went about to see to it that food was prepared for David. Then she and her servants carried it to David along with an apology for Nabal's actions. This action, on the part of Abigail, saved Nabal's life from the hand of David. God, however, had great displeasure of Nabal, who refused to help God's anointed leader, and shortly after the incident occurred, God ended Nabal's life:

1 Samuel 25:37-38
"But it came to pass in the morning, when the wine was gone out of Nabal, and his wife had told him these things, that his heart died within him, and he became as a stone. And it came to pass about ten days after, that YeHoVaH smote Nabal, that he died."

On the outside, to all who would perceive the possessions of Nabal, he seemed to have it all, however, Nabal's perception of the use of his blessings was very inconsistent with principles within the Word of God. Nabal did not perceive the times in which he lived and thus he missed God's hand on David. Nabal's wife, Abigail, understood God's hand and declared that to David, and in her apology for her husband's actions, she told David that her husband was as his name. Nabal means foolish. Nabal's refusal to help David was forgiven by David, as Abigail had asked, but we find shortly thereafter, Nabal dies by God's Hand.

Speaking of King David, he was a man who loved God and yet, he suffered greatly, especially under the hand of Saul, who tried to kill him, forcing him to live in caves and other desolate places in Israel. How many more Bible stories do you know of servants of God who, like David, suffered greatly? What about Moses, a man mightily used of God, at an early age, who chose to forsake the pomp and wealth of his position in Pharaoh's court.

Hebrews 11:24-27
"By faith Moses, when he was come to years, refused to be called the son of Pharaoh's daughter; Choosing rather to suffer affliction with the people of God, than to enjoy the pleasures of sin for a season; Esteeming the reproach of Christ greater riches than the treasures in Egypt: for he had respect unto the recompense of the reward. By faith he forsook Egypt, not fearing the wrath of the king: for he endured, as seeing him who is invisible."

Moses then left Egypt and lived a life of a nomad in the Midian. He married, had two sons, and then, after God called him to return to Egypt, he does so, first with his wife and son, but they later turn back. Moses completes God's assignment to bring out the children of Israel from Egypt, and if one looks at the life of Moses from that point until he death, there are no signs of great wealth for this man of God. Rather there are problems and trials beyond measure, yet this man knew God face to face!

Deuteronomy 34:10
"And there arose not a prophet since in Israel like unto Moses, whom YeHoVaH knew face to face."------

-----------------One can only perceive with the eye of the Spirit what that experience was to Moses. Certainly, this man, humble before God, was greatly blessed before God, but of his own personal wealth, we are told nothing.

God's goodness, biblically, may manifests in material blessings, but that is not a hard and fast rule. Yeshua understood there was a greater principle. On one occasion, Yeshua watched a woman who gave a donation to the temple. Her blessing to God followed the financial gift of a very rich man, yet Yeshua perceived her gift as far greater than the former man, who most likely followed the custom of the time, announcing his large gift with trumpet blasts. This incident we find recorded in the book of Luke:

Luke 21:1-6
"And he looked up and saw the rich men casting their gifts into the treasury. And he saw also a certain poor widow casting in two mites. And he said, Of a truth I say unto you, that this poor widow has cast in more than they all: For all these have of their abundance cast in unto the offerings of God: but she of her substance has cast in all the living that she had. And as some spoke of the temple, how it was adorned with goodly stones and gifts, he said, As for these things which you behold, the days will come, in the which there shall not be left one stone upon another, that shall not be thrown down."

This poor widow woman gave out of her necessities, therefore enacting her faith and trust in God to provide for her. The rich man gave from his abundance, which meant he did not give out of faith for God to provide for his needs. This man received the praise of men; however, the woman received the praise of God! Regarding the temple, both gifts, one from the rich man and one from the poor widow, went towards the building with its ornate decorations of gold, silver, and precious stones.

Soon that Temple was known throughout the world as one of the seven wonders, but on that day, the day the widow gave of her little offering, Yeshua proclaimed the Temple's destruction. The rich man first received his reward by those who saw his grand gift, but eventually it became lost in the Temple, which later was ultimately destroyed. The woman's small gift too became lost in the Temple and its inevitable destruction, but what about the reward of Yeshua's praise for her faith? Which person is still remembered with praise today, the rich man or the poor widow? Which gift, in God's eyes, had eternal value?

God, in His infinite mercy and goodness, rewards the gifts, such as those given in faith, like the widow woman, with blessings that last. David's faithfulness, long before he sat on the physical throne of Israel and collected great wealth for his son, Solomon, to build the temple, received blessings from God, including deliverance from every situation set up by his enemies to take his life. Yeshua's trust of God, in His submissive obedience to a death on the cross, having become sin, in the eyes of God, measured God's goodness, *not* by the opinions of those who looked at Him, either before or during His death, but rather, by God's pleasure in Him, even if it meant crushing Him as described in Isaiah 53.

CHAPTER'S SUMMARY

In this chapter, we looked at King David's declaration of God's goodness. Surely, that is one of the ways in which God recompenses His own; but by what circumstances does God release rewards from His goodness? Is it for reasons of noted valour alone, in the service of God, or is it rather, given to those whose heart is fixed upon YeHoVaH? Surely the latter is the truth, but many, today, perceive the former.

As a people of God, pressing into God for a move of His Hand in daily circumstances, as we examine the ways of God, so we may understand the One Who called us to such a great salvation, we can take a lesson from the ones we saw in this chapter. Let's remember David's love for God, even in circumstances pressing against him to take his life. In understanding the way of God's rewards, let's learn to ask God to help us look past the external signs we perceived. Let us remember that God looks at the humble heart that follows after Him, even in circumstances that, to onlookers, seem hard pressed to understand God's hand in it.

Let us also shift our focus to Yeshua, Who was despised and rejected by others. He was well acquainted with grief and sorrow, and that in the eyes of many did not point to one who is blessed by God. On the outside, His life, *if perceived only with the eyes of men,* showed outward signs of failure. He was, at the end of His life on earth, a condemned man, Who died with two criminals on either side of Him. Those with a human mindset certainly concluded His death was most shameful. Yet, through that death, God removed the sin of the world in one day and with the stripes on the back of Yeshua provided healing for all people.

Let us remember to look past the outward signs of a person's life, and not perceive God's blessings as a sign to indicate favour or disfavour with God. If we can embrace anything from this chapter, let it be that God desires we not look, especially to conclude something about another's life, by analyzing the outward circumstances. Let's learn and determine not to assess their blessings or lack thereof and conclude where they stand with God. Let's learn to keep our lips and the words of our mouth for God's praises!

In closing this chapter, let's keep before our eyes, this that the prophet declared:

Isaiah 55:9
"For as the heavens are higher than the earth, so are my ways higher than your ways, and my thoughts than your thoughts."

God's thoughts stretch far above those of man. His judgments, weighing circumstances, also hold higher values than those of human beings. His ways also coincide with His values, rather than those of natural man. His thoughts, of course, agree with His values, and thus He rewards in the way He sees best, to align with His plans and purposes, the sum of which no man really has revelation.

Therefore, when we see someone walking through trials, no matter the depth of that trial, let us remember that only God assesses all sides, for He alone has all the facts. A person's life, in God's eyes, and the character developed therein, is paramount. God alone knows the "gold" for which He digs, or the "dross" slated for removal. Situations in people's lives, no matter how much of it we think we see, or how much discernment we think we might possess, even after we have prayed and spent time with God, only God truly knows every part of it, from beginning to the end and He is not obliged to reveal it to anyone.

God desires that we understand His rewards for goodness, as described by Him within the Word, may look very different, touching circumstances which man's eyes cannot see. As God releases His Rewards, let us understand that they may come in circumstances that man's mind cannot possibly comprehend, and be for His specific purpose, originating from His perspective. God does not measure His Rewards in accordance with man's standards, and He does not reward in the same manner either. His eyes, alone, embrace the whole picture. Of this, and the following comment, we would do well to take note:

God's goodness towards men culminated in the person of His Son Yeshua, from Whom, with Whom and in Whom we receive the greatest rewards and the highest blessings.

God's rewards, as dispensed to man, originate beyond earth's standards and are therefore greater. Let's remember that in Messiah, we are recipients of the best God has to give!

WHEN UNVEILING HIS CHARACTER

8

"I will sing of the mercies of YeHoVaH for ever: with my mouth will I make known thy faithfulness to all generations. For I have said, Mercy shall be built up for ever: your faithfulness shall you establish in the very heavens. I have made a covenant with my chosen, I have sworn unto David my servant, Your seed will I establish for ever, and build up your throne to all generations. Selah."

Psalm 89:1-4

*T*O TRULY KNOW another person, it takes time. As situations arise in our life and as we walk through them with the ones we love, whether they are good of bad situations, each one shows us something about ourselves, and about those who either walk with us, or turn away from us. It could be said, then that each situation we experience in life, and walk through with those we know, reveals certain aspects of our being as well as shows the character of those near us. Only as time goes by do we know who we can truly count on and truly trust. The same thing applies as we get to know God, and see His character revealed to us.

When we first experience salvation, as we approach God with a brokenness over our sinfulness, we walk through an open door, not only to attain eternal redemption, but also to know God. We thus become privileged to call Him Abba, Father:

Galatians 4:6-7
"And because you are sons, God has sent forth the Spirit of his Son into your hearts, crying, Abba, Father. Wherefore you are no more a servant, but a son; and if a son, then an heir of God through Christ."

As we walk out our lives, from salvation onward, it is God's intention that we understand He is our Father, and we are more than a servant. We are a "son", an heir of God through Messiah. The term "son" here is a generic term which refers to both male and female believers. Its application is very simple: as a believer we belong to God and hence are adopted into His family.

Romans 8:15
"For you have not received the spirit of bondage again to fear; but you have received the Spirit of adoption, whereby we cry, Abba, Father."

With a relationship now established between the Father and His child, we have opportunity to understand the One we call Father. As any good earthly father wishes his child to know his love and care for them, even more so does our Heavenly Father. Thus, if we truly desire to know God, He will lead us through open doors, whereby He unveils His character to us. All we need is a willingness to listen to the voice of the Holy Spirit, as He leads and guides us in our knowledge of God. In every situation we face, whether we classify it as good or bad, if we are willing to see it, God will reveal His character to us so that we can intimately know the God we have chosen as our Lord and Saviour. This is how the saints of old knew God, and this is how we get to know Him too.

In our opening scripture, the Psalmist, Ethan the Ezrahite, makes a statement about God:

Psalm 89:1-4
"I will sing of the mercies of YeHoVaH for ever: with my mouth will I make known your faithfulness to all generations. For I have said, Mercy shall be built up for ever: your faithfulness shall you establish in the very heavens. I

have made a covenant with my chosen, I have sworn unto David my servant, Your seed will I establish for ever, and build up your throne to all generations. Selah."

First, this Psalmist knew God. Personally, he considered his own life, as well as looked at God's dealings with Israel. In those dealings, he saw God's mercies. "Mercy" in Hebrew is a rather interesting word:

Mercy	Strong's # 2617	חסד
	from 2616	khaw sad
Strong's Concordance[36] says that "חסד" is used 248 times. 149 times it has been interpreted as Mercy; 40 times as Kindness, 30 times as Lovingkindness, 12 times as goodness, 5 times as kindly, 4 times as merciful, 3 times as favour, and 1 time as good, goodliness, pity, and then in a negative sense once as reproach and once as a wicked thing.		

The Hebrew Word picture shows us a deeper meaning. "ח" shows us a walling out. "ס" shows a just discipline or sentence for behaviour, thus the parent root shows a walling out of a just discipline or sentence for behaviour. "ד", the child root, shows what enters the door of the life is different than what is deserved.

---

[36] Sourced from onlinebible.net.

Mercy, then, pushes back, or walls out, or keeps away the just punishment. That same idea reaches out to show lovingkindness, goodness, etc.

Did Israel know God's Mercy? In other words, did Israel experience a lesser just punishment than what her actions required? What about individuals throughout the Word of God? Did they receive less than their actions deserved? A resounding "Yes" can be said as an answer to the questions above. So grateful, therefore, was the Psalmist, that he would sing of the mercies of YeHoVaH. Then he speaks of God's faithfulness, which originates from the Hebrew word "faith":

Faith	Strong's # 0530	אצומנ
	from 0539	em-oo-naw
Strong's shows this word as meaning AV-faithfulness, carrying the idea of fidelity, steadfastness or steadiness.		

The Hebrew word picture personifies faith as a strong leader "א" who comes alongside a person, in all matters of life "מ", for the purpose of joining with that person "ו" to bring about their inheritance "מ" via their surrender to God's Spirit "ה".

In reference to God's faithfulness, it shows God's strength to get us through every situation that we face in life. He is there with us, never leaving nor forsaking us, helping us to surrender to His Spirit so we can receive the best from the situation. That best, of course, aligns with God's eternal plans for us.

No matter what happens to us in this life, God is never caught by surprise. He is prepared for everything and along side His children, ever ready to bring them what they need for victory in that situation. This aspect of God's character we can count on! Consider, one more thing too! Everything that touches our life, God promises to somehow turn for good:

Romans 8:28
"And we know that all things work together for good to them that love God, to them who are the called according to his purpose."

Referring to the Psalmist, Paul, the Apostle, desired that all generations know God's faithful, supporting character. "Mercy shall be built up forever: thy faithfulness shalt thou establish in the very heavens". In other words, as another Psalmist decreed:

Psalm 136:1-26
"O give thanks unto YeHoVaH; for [he is] good: for his mercy [endures] for ever. O give thanks unto the God of

gods: for his mercy [endures] for ever. O give thanks to YeHoVaH of lords: for his mercy [endures] for ever. To him who alone does great wonders: for his mercy [endure] for ever. To him that by wisdom made the heavens: for his mercy [endures] for ever. To him that stretched out the earth above the waters: for his mercy [endures] for ever. To him that made great lights: for his mercy [endures] for ever: The sun to rule by day: for his mercy [endures] for ever: The moon and stars to rule by night: for his mercy [endures] for ever."

"To him that smote Egypt in their firstborn: for his mercy [endures] for ever: And brought out Israel from among them: for his mercy [endures] for ever: With a strong hand, and with a stretched-out arm: for his mercy [endures] for ever. To him which divided the Red sea into parts: for his mercy [endures] for ever: And made Israel to pass through the midst of it: for his mercy [endures] for ever: But overthrew Pharaoh and his host in the Red sea: for his mercy [endures] for ever. To him which led his people through the wilderness: for his mercy [endures] for ever. To him which smote great kings: for his mercy [endures]] for ever: 18 And slew famous kings: for his mercy [endures] for ever: Sihon king of the Amorites: for his mercy [endures] for ever: And Og the king of Bashan: for his mercy [endures] for ever: And gave their land for an heritage: for his mercy [endures] for ever: [Even] an heritage unto Israel his servant: for his mercy [endures] for ever."

"Who remembered us in our low estate: for his mercy [endures] for ever: And has redeemed us from our enemies: for his mercy [endures] for ever. Who gives food to all flesh: for his mercy [endures] for ever. O give thanks unto the God of heaven: for his mercy [endures] for ever."

In reading this Psalm 136, we note that the author rehearses important events of the earth, and God's mercy in that regard. He speaks of creation, specifically mentioning God's mercy regarding the heavens, including the sun, the moon and the stars. This great order that God placed in the heavens, the Psalmist considered signs of God's mercy. The Psalmist also rehearsed important events in Israel's history too. Events such as the great deliverance from Egypt, as God's hand parted the sea, giving Israel an escape from Pharaoh's wrath, when he determined to kill them. He considered their entrance into Canaan Land and God's mighty Hand which made them a powerful nation under King David. Whether in want or in plenty, the Psalmist saw God's mercy at work.

To summarize what both Psalmists say, God's mercy, which is part of His character, has been seen in every aspect of Israel's existence, even going further back, to the very act of creation, where God's mercy was clearly demonstrated in the heavens. This demonstration is for no other purpose than to show all mankind that someone exists that is far greater than man, someone who made all the heavens and the earth. That is what the Psalms tell us:

Psalm 19:1
"The heavens declare the glory of God; and the firmament shows his handywork."

That is just one aspect of God's Mercy as seen in the heavens. That same Psalm, in its following verses show us even more:

Psalm 19:2-4 a)
"Day unto day utters speech, and night unto night shows knowledge. There is no speech nor language, where their voice is not heard. Their line is gone out through all the earth, and their words to the end of the world."

As a person looks towards the heavens, they will find a message in the very essence of the heavens. That message speaks of God as its creator. It does not matter what language of earth the person speaks; the heavens speak from one end of the earth to another of its glorious message. If one understood their message, understood their original names, then they would know the plan of Salvation as it is shown in the heavens, displayed in the stars. Is this not mercy to call man to a greater, far higher, loftier being who made all these things!

In other words, God has placed aspects of His Mercy throughout this universe in which we dwell. Our hearts and minds need only be open to it and if we desire it to be so, we will hear its message. We all need God's mercy in order to be saved. Prior to our salvation we may taste of it, here and there, as God's mercy touches our lives, but we won't truly touch the depths of that mercy until we taste of it through the avenue of our personal salvation. Then, we will know it by experience.

This is how we know any aspect of God, by personally partaking of it. One won't know God's Healing power until they are not well. One won't know God's provision, until their own fails. One won't know God's deliverance until every other door closes. One won't know God's peace until they experience chaos. The list goes on and on of things about God, that man will never know, unless through that situation, they turn it all over to God, to see His Hand move. Then comes the revelation of God, through that circumstance as He enters it and by the power of the Holy Spirit, unveils a specific aspect of God's Character to us.

In our hour of need, standing ready to learn more of God, that very situation is an awesome invitation to draw near to God. From that drawing near, a fruit develops, which is more precious than at any other time in our life. It is at those times when we learn to experience God's compassion, His love and mercy, His wisdom and His counsel and many other various aspects of our wonderful God, unveiled before our eyes. Through that situation, one we most likely would never desire, comes the most intimate look at our God.

As human beings, we like everything that touches our life to be comforting. We do not welcome grief, sorrow, or any form of troublesome times. Each one of us, if given the choice, would probably refuse most, if not all, of the difficult situations in life. However, we need to remember, that each situation that knocks on our door presents itself with certain opportunities, some of which may help us to release any dross God desires to bring to the surface.

Also, we can look forward to an unveiling of God's character as He comes to us at that time of need and brings forth the answer. Each even in our life, if we allow it, is like a pair of eyeglasses. Putting them on, we see a revelation of our inner being as well as perceive certain characteristics of our majestic God as He reaches into our circumstances to help us. Ours is but to make a choice, whether to unwrap the whole package in front of us, or not. We alone chose to look beneath the outside wrapper to seek God for the beautiful fruit that lay hidden within the unwanted circumstance, part of which brings forth a closeness from drawing nearer to Him, using the opportunity to know Him more intimately.

CHAPTER'S SUMMARY

As we walked through this chapter, we looked at two Psalmists and their view on mercy. We saw that God designed the very heavens above us so that we can know Him. Its voice calls to us and speaks to us of Him and of His unlimited compassion. Surely, as we look to those heavens, those spaces that are displayed as far greater than we and are open to its basic message of a creator with great mercy, for He is indeed far greater than we, and even far greater than the heavens which He created. Our problems are small, like the grains of sand on the seashore. His ability to resolve them is much higher than the distance from the earth to the farthest point in the heavens.

We also discussed our need to remember that through every circumstance that touches our life, God calls to His Children to draw near to Him. Then, through that circumstance, He will unveil His character, His very person so we may know Him and not just His Ways. His faithfulness to unveil His character to us is like a mountain standing tall in front of us, inviting us to take the risk and climb up to a higher place in Him. We need only take the invitation, allowing Him to hold our hand as we walk through to the other side of the storm in victory.

Let's remember that every circumstance we face, whether good of bad, is a wonderful and rare opportunity to walk through a door to realize an intimate relationship with God where He will unveil His very character to us:

HOW GOD UNVEILS HIMSELF
If we face fear, as we seek God, He shows **us His face of Love:**

1 John 4:18
"There is no fear in love; but perfect love casts out fear: because fear hath torment. He that fears is not made perfect in love."

If we face sickness, as we seek God, He shows us **His face of healing:**

Psalm 103:1-5
"Bless YeHoVaH, O my soul: and all that is within me, bless his holy name. Bless YeHoVaH, O my soul, and forget not all his benefits: Who forgives all your iniquities; who heals all your diseases; Who redeems your life from destruction; who crowns you with lovingkindness and tender mercies; Who satisfies your mouth with good things; so that your youth is renewed like the eagle's."

Psalm 147:1-5
"Praise YeHoVaH: for it is good to sing praises unto our God; for it is pleasant; and praise is lovely. YeHoVaH does build up Jerusalem: he gathers together the outcasts of Israel. He heals the broken in heart, and binds up their wounds. He tells the number of the stars; he calls them all by their names. Great is our Lord, and of great power: his understanding is infinite."

If we face stress, as we seek God, He shows us **His face of Peace:**

John 14:27
"Peace I leave with you, my peace I give unto you: not as the world gives, give I unto you. Let not your heart be troubled, neither let it be afraid."

If we face financial concerns or any kind of lack, as we seek God, He shows us **His face as Provider**, and we'll know that man does not live by bread alone.

Genesis 22:14
"And Abraham called the name of that place Jehovahjireh: as it is said to this day, In the mount of YeHoVaH it shall be seen."

Matthew 4:4
"But he answered and said, It is written, Man shall not live by bread alone, but by every word that proceeds out of the mouth of God."

If we face abandonment, and seek God, He shows us **the face of Yahweh Shammah.** (YeHoVaH is there! It is about His Presence!)

Ezekiel 48:35
"It was round about eighteen thousand measures: and the name of the city from that day shall be, YeHoVaH is there."

1 Chronicles 16:27
"Glory and honour are in his presence; strength and gladness are in his place."

If we face oppression, as we seek Him, we'll see **His face of Deliverance:**

Luke 4:18-19
"The Spirit of YeHoVaH is upon me, because he has anointed me to preach the gospel to the poor; he has sent me to heal the brokenhearted, to preach deliverance to the captives, and recovering of sight to the blind, to set at liberty them that are bruised, To preach the acceptable year of YeHoVaH."

Psalm 32:7
"You art my hiding place; You shall preserve me from trouble; you shall compass me about with songs of deliverance. Selah. "

If we face opposition, as we seek God, He will show us **His Face as YeHoVaH of Hosts**:

Psalm 68:1-4
"Let God arise, let his enemies be scattered: let them also that hate him flee before him. As smoke is driven away, so drive them away: as wax melts before the fire, so let the wicked perish at the presence of God. But let the righteous be glad; let them rejoice before God: yea, let them exceedingly rejoice. Sing unto God, sing praises to his name: extol him that rides upon the heavens by his name JAH, and rejoice before him."

If we face situations where we need discernment and clarity, as we seek God, He will show us **His Face of Revelation** (as well as understanding):

Daniel 2:20-23
"Daniel answered and said, Blessed be the name of God for ever and ever: for wisdom and might are his: And he changes the times and the seasons: he removes kings, and sets up kings: he gives wisdom unto the wise, and knowledge to them that know understanding: He reveals the deep and secret things: he knows what is in the darkness, and the light dwells with him. I thank you, and praise you, O God of my fathers,

who has given me wisdom and might, and has made known unto me now what we desired of you: for you have now made known unto us the king's matter."

If we face situations with death, and we seek God, He will show us **His face of Resurrection and Eternal life**:

Hosea 13:14
"I will ransom them from the power of the grave; I will redeem them from death: O death, I will be your plagues; O grave, I will be your destruction: repentance shall be hid from my eyes."

John 5:39
"Search the scriptures; for in them you think you have eternal life: and they are they which testify of me."

Let us learn to embrace the ways of YeHoVaH, including this way, as we invite God into our circumstances to help us through them, no matter how difficult, or even how often we need to call upon Him. Let us remember that one of God's ways is to unveil His character in the things in our life. We only need to walk through the open door.

**In every situation we face,
may we lift our eyes above the experience.
Let's remember to seek God and
look for a revelation of His character!**

BEFORE CHAPTER 9

Humankind, in general, does not understand how one person, upon this earth, seemingly sails through life, almost unscathed by negative circumstances, while another seems to drown in a life of frequent sorrows. People with and without a faith-life form theories. These theories try to define why trouble comes to a person; what caused it; why one person receives a problem, and another receives a blessing. Such theories are numerous, and often based on what people consider good, sound biblical teaching.

As we approach the subject of how God dispenses His purpose, we'll speak on "trials and tribulations", as these, in one form or another, touch every human being. In discussing this subject, to ensure both author and reader are on the same page, this chapter introduction sets out certain factors to show the author's approach to the subject of tribulation, however, since we can not speak about every theory in this regard, there's only a generalized view related here.

Please understand, the author believes that God is the only one who really knows the totality of *why* things happen to any individual. These reasons God may well reveal to the person going through the trial, or perhaps to others, close to that individual, to help them through to the other side. God, however, is not the author of sickness, disease, or any form of physical ailment. These things arrive in a person's life from a source other than God.

Furthermore, it is God's pleasure to see them removed from a person's life. Therefore, as we discuss tribulation, and the lives of certain biblical characters who experienced great measures of it, we'll look at how each saint looked to God, through their trial and how God produced something good from their time of trouble. This is, therefore, a biblical approach:

Romans 8:28
"And we know that all things work together for good to them that love God, to them who are the called according to his purpose."

In conclusion then, the following chapter discusses God's purpose and how it is revealed in our lives, through the events that touch us. Therefore, in reading this chapter, we'll speak of "tribulation", as a word to summarize any form of distress, conflict, discomfort, or suffering that touches one's life. There are various reasons why these arise, one of which is simply because we live in a fallen world. When tribulation is shown as touching a life, we'll approach that topic from the viewpoint that *God allowed it*. His reasons for allowing it may vary, depending on the individual and the purpose or reason for which God permitted it.

In reading this chapter, please keep this in mind, that God loves mankind deeply and has an unbending, unyielding love for all, which even increases towards His children. As we live in a fallen world, anyone, at any time, can find themselves in any form of tribulation. No matter what that situation, however, God understands it from its very beginning to its end, but we don't!

Therefore, since our human thinking cannot possibly grasp God's plans and purposes, we must raise our sights to higher ground, looking to stay close to Him and walk through each and every situation we face, looking to Him for wisdom and insights. With our eyes upon Him, our trust positioned also in Him, we know we can get to the other side, and perhaps, with His help and revelation, even know the purpose for which the thing touched our lives.

WHEN DISPENSING HIS PURPOSE

9

"Hold your peace, let me alone, that I may speak, and let come on me what will. Wherefore do I take my flesh in my teeth, and put my life in my hand? Though he slay me, yet will I trust in him: but I will maintain my own ways before him."

Job 13:13-15

JOB, THE PERSON speaking in the above scripture, finds himself in a very difficult situation. As he tries to make some sense of it, he simply cannot. In his frustration, he turns to his friends to speak to him hoping for some insight, perhaps even for some comfort. Yet, his friends speak only about how Job must somehow be at fault. Surely, his friends believe, that somewhere, somehow, Job offended God and those offences caused Job's present condition. At one point in their rather long deliberation, Job tells them, "Be quiet. Leave me alone so I can speak. Let happen to me what will.[37]"

Next, Job uses a proverbial expression for his time, which in modern language means, "I risk everything to say this, perhaps even taking my life in my hands, but, though He slay me, yet will I trust Him: but I will maintain (correct) my ways before Him".

Job's suffering indeed had a root cause, but that cause was not Job's offensive behaviour before YeHoVaH. Job actually pleased God. We hear that as the book of Job opens:

Job 1:1
"There was a man in the land of Uz, whose name was Job; and that man was perfect and upright, and one that feared God, and turned away from evil."

Nevertheless, a trial, initiated by ha satan, touched Job's life.

---

[37] Author's interpretation of part of the scripture above

Job 1:9-12
"Then ha satan answered YeHoVaH, and said, Does Job fear God for nought? Have you not made a hedge about him, and about his house, and about all that he has on every side? you have blessed the work of his hands, and his substance is increased in the land. But put forth your hand now, and touch all that he has, and he will curse you to your face. And YeHoVaH said unto ha satan, Behold, all that he has is in your power; only upon himself put not forth your hand. So ha satan went forth from the presence of YeHoVaH."

With God's permission to touch Job's life and the precious things which he possessed, ha satan, (the adversary),[38] went about his evil tasks. Death came to Job's sons, and eventually, Job lost almost everything, except for his wife, which ha satan used to speak for him. She advised Job to curse God and die. Yet, throughout Job's difficult trial, he never yielded to any temptation uttered by his wife, or any other, to curse God. Even though he did not understand why things happened to him, he remained faithful to God. Even when God allowed almost all that Job loved and possessed to go from him, and even when Job's body was wracked with painful disease, he still chose to bless God and remain a faithful servant to Him.

---

[38] In Hebrew, the word our English language interprets as satan" means adversary and therefore does not need a capital letter.

Job, as well as many other great people in the Bible experienced horrible trials. Among them: Naomi, who lost her husband, her two sons and all they possessed. So bitter was her sorrow she changed her name from "Naomi", which means my delight, to "Mara" which means bitterness. Yet, this woman remained faithful to her God and through the blessing of a daughter-in-law named Ruth, came a son from whose seed, eventually, came King David.

King David, also, has great tribulation under the hand of King Saul, who persecuted David. During the time of that persecution, his first wife was taken from him by Saul. David had no home to call his own, due to circumstances causing him to flee for his life. He lived in caves and wandered in the wilderness of Israel.

Often David was hungry and frustrated with the relentless pursuit by Saul, a pursuit aimed to remove David from the face of the earth. Yet, David did nothing to cause the persecution, nor anything to harm Saul, who had become his enemy. Instead, David waited for God to resolve the situation, even though it took years.

Joseph, the 11th child of Jacob, suffered enormous suffering. He was thrown into a pit by his brothers, sold into slavery, tossed into prison for an accusation of adultery of which he was not guilty. Of Joseph, Psalm 105 says:

Psalm 105:16-22
"Moreover he called for a famine upon the land: he broke the whole staff of bread. He sent a man before them, even Joseph, who was sold for a servant: Whose feet they hurt with fetters: he was laid in iron: Until the time that his word came: the word of YeHoVaH tried him. The king sent and loosed him; even the ruler of the people and let him go free. He made him lord of his house, and ruler of all his substance: To bind his princes at his pleasure; and teach his senators wisdom."

There are many more saints of the Old and New Testament that we could add to this list of those who suffered greatly, yet their affliction came without any apparent cause, nor fault of their own. Their tribulation, even when extremely challenging, brought forth something amazing. In other words, they overcame.

Regarding that subject of overcoming, Yeshua said:

John 16:33
"These things I have spoken unto you, that in me you might have peace. In the world you shall have tribulation: but be of good cheer; I have overcome the world."

As Yeshua spoke these words to His Disciples, He was about to undergo a tribulation like no other man. In fact, that coming trial to Yeshua was so strong that, even in thinking about it, Yeshua's body went into deep distress:

Matthew 26:36-39
"Then comes Jesus with them unto a place called Gethsemane, and said unto the disciples, Sit here, while I go and pray yonder. And he took with him Peter and the two sons of Zebedee, and began to be sorrowful and very heavy. Then said he unto them, My soul is exceeding sorrowful, even unto death: tarry here, and watch with me. And he went a little further, and fell on his face, and prayed, saying, O my Father, if it be possible, let this cup pass from me: nevertheless not as I will, but as you will."

Yeshua, in this time of His life, was about to endure a trial so difficult, it stressed His body. Yet, even knowing what was to happen, Yeshua faced the situation by accepting the Father's will, over that of His own, saying, "Nevertheless, not as I will, but as you will".

Did Yeshua understand something about suffering that we do not know today? Surely He knew the words of the prophet, Isaiah, which spoke of His time of suffering. A review of that passage in Isaiah gives us highlights of His suffering. Let's look at this scripture, picking out *only what He suffered*:[39]

Isaiah 53:1-9
"1 Who has believed our report? and to whom is the arm of YeHoVaH revealed?"

His godly message was rejected. Few knew He was the Messiah.

"2 For he shall grow up before him as a tender plant, and as a root out of a dry ground: he has no form nor comeliness; and when we shall see him, [there is] no beauty that we should desire him."

As He grew up, He was like a tender plant, but He grew out of dry ground, meaning he grew up in hard times. He was not good looking, so that people looked at Him and desired anything from Him because of his good looks. (In today's words, He was not a handsome man.) There was nothing out of the ordinary to draw you to such a man.

"3 He is despised and rejected of men; a man of sorrows and acquainted with grief: and we hid as it were [our] faces from him; he was despised, and we esteemed him not."

---

[39] Scripture verse in bold, author's comment in italics.

When people looked at Yeshua, they despised Him. He knew rejection. He knew sorrow and grief very well. There was no person to comfort Him, for people turned away from Him. They despised Him and esteemed Him (His life) of no value.

"4 Surely he has borne our griefs and carried our sorrows: yet we did esteem him stricken, smitten of God, and afflicted."

He carried our griefs, (the horrible griefs that mankind could suffer.) He carried every sorrow, but people looked at Him and considered God afflicted Him because, they thought, He led a sinful life.

"5 But he [was] wounded for our transgressions, [he was] bruised for our iniquities: the chastisement of our peace [was] upon him; and with his stripes we are healed."

Looking at only His suffering, in this verse we see His body wounded, bruised, and the stripes of the Roman whip afflicted His body. (Yet, He did this all for us!)

"6 All we like sheep have gone astray; we have turned every one to his own way; and YeHoVaH has laid on him the iniquity of us all."

Upon His Body, all iniquity was laid upon Him. (Think about a person who knew no sin, who God made sin! What suffering for the Holy Son of God!)

"7 He was oppressed, and he was afflicted, yet he opened not his mouth: he is brought as a lamb to the slaughter, and as a sheep before her shearers is silent, so he opened not his mouth."

He stood before accusers who railed horrible accusations against Him, yet He did not speak one word in His own defence. (What mental, physical, and emotional suffering He endured!)

"8 He was taken from prison and from judgment: and who shall declare his generation? for he was cut off out of the land of the living: for the transgression of my people was he stricken."

Treated like a criminal, He faced a judgment which was unfair, and His end, for a man in His prime, was a very undeserved, unfair death, condemned as a criminal!)

"9 And he made his grave with the wicked, and with the rich in his death; because he had done no violence, neither [was any] deceit in his mouth."

He died with criminals. His body was laid to rest in a tomb given to Him by a rich man. Yet He was not a violent man, nor one who was deceitful. This is clear evidence of suffering, marked as someone evil, not deemed even worthy of living life here on earth.

While it is true that Yeshua did all this for our salvation, if we take some time to look at the very suffering, we see that He knew deep, intense rejection on every level of human existence. Yet, He never sinned through it all. He rather yielded His whole being to serve the ultimate purpose of YeHoVaH. God's ultimate purpose of this suffering we embrace because we see the end which was our salvation. In looking at Yeshua, however, as He went through this ordeal, God's people at the time, did not understand the depth of God's plan. Yeshua, in His wisdom understood and looked past the suffering to something else:

Hebrews 12:1-3
"Wherefore seeing we also are compassed about with so great a cloud of witnesses, let us lay aside every weight, and the sin which does so easily beset us, and let us run with patience the race that is set before us, Looking unto Jesus the author and finisher of our faith; who for the joy that was set before him endured the cross, despising the shame[40], and is set

---

[40] Bolding and italics not in original text

down at the right hand of the throne of God. For consider him that endured such contradiction of sinners against himself, lest you be wearied and faint in your minds."

Yeshua's heart, mind and soul focused on the purpose of the Father, in doing His will. That was His delight. Indeed, Yeshua knew heart ache, tribulation and many other things that pressed against Him, yet through it all, He trusted His Father, and the Father's purpose. Is it possible that we, who follow Yeshua, need to do the same?

Whether we like to receive it or prefer to resist any idea of tribulation touching our life, surely it originates from the fallen world in which we live. Christians are not exempt from suffering persecution nor heartache, nor tribulation. After all, if our own Lord and Master suffered greatly, suffering in a manner far beyond all our possible understanding, why should we see ourselves exempt?

Perhaps, we should rather look at the purpose of God in allowing anything to touch our lives. Maybe God sees some behaviour in us, He wants removed and only a particular hardship will do the job. Perhaps God wants to use that circumstance to show Himself as God to onlookers? The fact is, we don't know why "bad things happen to good people". Neither Job, nor his friends understood that either! Perhaps it is time, that we, as believers, need to look past the outward appearance of any situation to see God at work, and God's purpose.

When speaking of God's purpose, we must understand that the thoughts and counsels of God are far higher than we normally think. We need to draw near to Him, in every trial, in every tribulation, to ask Him His purpose. He might reveal it, but it is possible, He might not tell us. At times, we need to simply walk by faith and put our trust in the One we call Lord. Job, did that, as did Naomi, David and many other saints in the Bible, saints who did not necessarily understand the purpose of God:

Hebrews 11:17-40
"By faith Abraham, when he was tried, offered up Isaac: and he that had received the promises offered up his only begotten [son], Of whom it was said, That in Isaac shall your seed be called: Accounting that God [was] able to raise [him] up, even from the dead; from where also he received him in a figure."

"By faith Isaac blessed Jacob and Esau concerning things to come. By faith Jacob, when he was a dying, blessed both the sons of Joseph; and worshipped, [leaning] upon the top of his staff. By faith Joseph, when he died, made mention of the departing of the children of Israel; and gave commandment concerning his bones. By faith Moses, when he was born,

was hid three months of his parents, because they saw [he was] a proper child; and they were not afraid of the king's commandment. By faith Moses, when he was come to years, refused to be called the son of Pharaoh's daughter; Choosing rather to suffer affliction with the people of God, than to enjoy the pleasures of sin for a season; Esteeming the reproach of Christ greater riches than the treasures in Egypt: for he had respect unto the recompense of the reward. By faith he forsook Egypt, not fearing the wrath of the king: for he endured, as seeing him who is invisible. Through faith he kept the Passover, and the sprinkling of blood, lest he that destroyed the firstborn should touch them."

"By faith they passed through the Red sea as by dry [land]: which the Egyptians assaying to do were drowned. By faith the walls of Jericho fell down, after they were compassed about seven days. By faith the harlot Rahab perished not with them that believed not, when she had received the spies with peace."

"And what shall I more say? for the time would fail me to tell of Gedeon, and [of] Barak, and [of] Samson, and [of] Jephthae; [of] David also, and Samuel, and [of] the prophets: Who through faith subdued kingdoms, brought righteousness, obtained promises, stopped the mouths of lions, Quenched the violence of fire, escaped the edge of the sword, out of weakness were made strong, waxed valiant in fight, turned to flight the armies of the aliens. Women received their dead raised to life again: and others were

tortured, not accepting deliverance; that they might obtain a better resurrection."

"And others had trial of [cruel] mockings and scourgings, yes, moreover of bonds and imprisonment: They were stoned, they were sawn asunder, were tempted, were slain with the sword: they wandered about in sheepskins and goatskins; being destitute, afflicted, tormented; (Of whom the world was not worthy:) they wandered in deserts, and [in] mountains, and [in] dens and caves of the earth."

"And these all, having obtained a good report through faith, received not the promise: God having provided some better thing for us, that they without us should not be made perfect."

Each saint mentioned in these scriptures lived by faith, some receiving the promises while living on earth, while others did not. Some saints they stoned, sawed in two. These saints were tempted, murdered by the sword, wandered about in rags, destitute, afflicted, and tormented. These believers, Hebrews says, were people of whom the world was not worthy. These saints lived in a place with God, living for a purpose unseen by those who gaze at them with a worldly point of view. These worldly onlookers do not grasp the situation, at its core. Nor do they grasp God's greater purpose, one that purpose came through trials and tribulations.

Perhaps these suffering saints understood one of God's ways of attaining His Purposes, which at times, arise through trials and tribulations. Perhaps, they did not. Whatever they understood individually, we don't know, but this we know and can trust as we look at God and not the circumstances:

Jeremiah 29:11
"For I know the thoughts that I think toward you, says YeHoVaH, thoughts of peace, and not of evil, to give you an expected end."

CHAPTER'S SUMMARY

Throughout this chapter we spoke about men and women of faith who endured trials and suffering, who allowed God to accomplish His purpose in their life, and through their life in the avenue of God's choice. We briefly touched on the life of Naomi, King David, and Joseph, as well as Job. We saw how they trusted God, no matter the circumstance, and once on the other side of their trial, even if they did not understand, they recognized God's greater purpose. We even looked at the suffering of Yeshua, to see what He endured on our behalf. Through that endurance, came God's ultimate purpose of Salvation for the entire world.

We can see, therefore, from the lives of the many individuals we studied, that God is far greater than anything that touches His children's life, and through it, He can produce a greater purpose. The key to seeing that purpose produced is simply this: learn to love YeHoVaH with all our heart, mind, soul and strength and our neighbour as ourselves. In that way, our value system remains aligned with God's and produces good fruit for us, as well as for God's kingdom.

No matter what touches our life, as we go through anything, let's remember that God has made us more than conquerors, and each situation, whether we know its purpose before, during or after, produces fruit for God's Kingdom, including a greater knowledge and deeper relationship with the One we call God!

Romans 8:35-39
"Who shall separate us from the love of Christ? shall tribulation, or distress, or persecution, or famine, or nakedness, or peril, or sword? As it is written, For your sake we are killed all the day long; we are accounted as sheep for the slaughter. No, in all these things we are more than conquerors through him that loved us. For I am persuaded, that neither death, nor life, nor angels, nor principalities, nor powers, nor things present, nor things to come, Nor height, nor depth, nor any other creature, shall be able to separate us from the love of God, which is in Christ Jesus our Lord."

Let us learn to seek God's Wisdom in everything that touches our lives, looking beyond our human thoughts to a higher plane of God's greater purpose as it may just bring great blessing to God and man!

WHEN REVEALING HIS GLORY

10

"And he said, My presence shall go with you, and I will give you rest. And he said unto him, If your presence go not with me, carry us not up from here. For wherein shall it be known here that I and your people have found grace in thy sight? is it not in that you go with us? so shall we be separated, I and your people, from all the people that are upon the face of the earth."

Exodus 33:14-16

*T*HERE IS MUCH desire, amongst God's people today, to experience the Manifest Presence of YeHoVaH. Many believers long to go past the Manifest Presence of God as they long for an appearance of the Shekinah glory of God. In this chapter, we will look at these two very important topics: The Manifest Presence of God and the Shekinah glory. Remember, as we look at these two topics, we are looking for the Ways of YeHoVaH.

THE MANIFEST PRESENCE OF GOD

Our English word "manifest" means to make visible; give evidence or proof of a certain thing. Connecting this word with the presence of God, it means there is some sort of evidence that God is in our midst. Many Christians, especially when in worship, believe their spiritual sensitivities allow them to recognize the Presence of God. God is everywhere but when a person senses God's Presence, they simply become aware of God's Presence, where earlier it was not noticeable. This thinking is in accordance with the Bible:

Psalm 139:7
"Where shall I go from your spirit? or where shall I flee from your presence?"

Even in First Covenant times, King David knew that God's Presence was inescapable. As the Psalm continues, his thoughts go to those desolate, troubling places upon this earth, places where he lived earlier, yet, no matter the circumstances, God's Presence was still there:

Psalm 139:8-12
"If I ascend up into heaven, you are there: if I make my bed in hell, behold, you are there. If I take the wings of the morning, and dwell in the uttermost parts of the sea; Even there shall your hand lead me, and your right hand shall hold me. If I say, Surely the darkness shall cover me; even the night shall be light about me. Yes, the darkness hides not from you; but the night shines as the day: the darkness and the light are both alike to you."

King David concluded that heaven, even with its infinite space, can never take him away from God's Presence. Even if his life took him to the lowest pit of hell, God's Presence is still there. If David suddenly sprouted wings and flew to the uttermost parts of the Sea, not even then, could he escape God's Presence. If somehow David became wrapped in total darkness, God's Presence is still there, and God's vision, not impaired by darkness, sees it all. God sees just as clearly in the dark as in bright sunlight.

Regarding God's Presence, then, our first solid biblical truth is that God's Presence is everywhere. When one recognizes that Presence of God, they simply become aware of what is always there. There is, however, a presence of God which, when manifested, is not simply sensed, but it is rather visible.

SHEKINAH GLORY OF GOD

This word "shekinah", as a noun, does not appear in the Bible. Instead, we have the verb form:

Shekinah	Noun Strong's # 7931[41]	שׁכן
	(It is a primitive root)	shaw khan (verb)
It means to settle down, to abide, to tabernacle.		

Examples of the verb usage is in the following scriptures:

Exodus 24:16
"And the glory of YeHoVaH abode <7931> upon mount Sinai, and the cloud covered it six days: and the seventh day he called unto Moses out of the midst of the cloud."

Exodus 40:35
"And Moses was not able to enter into the tent of the congregation, because the cloud abode <7931> thereon, and the glory of YeHoVaH filled the tabernacle."

Both these scriptures refer to a visible Presence of God, and is what Jewish Rabbis labelled, the Shekinah Glory of God. According to what some Rabbis teach, the word means dwelling or settling, thus, they believe

---
[41] Sourced from onlinebible.net.

YeHoVaH came and dwelt in their midst, manifesting His Presence in that Shekinah glory.

When the Bible records the manifestation of the cloud over Solomon's Temple at its dedication, it uses another word:

Glory	Strong's # 3519[42]	כבוד
	(a primitive root)	kaw-bode
It means glory, splendour, honour and in Hebrew suggests a heaviness or weightiness.		

In our earlier scripture from Exodus 24:26, the word "כבוד (kaw-bode), Strong's # 3519, appears:

Exodus 24:16
"And the glory <3519> of YeHoVaH abode <7931> upon mount Sinai, and the cloud covered it six days: and the seventh day he called unto Moses out of the midst of the cloud."

Rabbis, for centuries, believed this manifestation, at the dedication of Solomon's Temple, was in fact, the same manifestation of God as He, earlier, brought about during the time of the Tabernacle in the wilderness. As

---

[42] Sourced from onlinebible.net.

these Rabbis explain the Presence of God, they relate that its manifestation shows a visible sign of the Person of God dwelling in their midst.

Hence, in Jewish understanding, God came down in person to dwell with the people in the time of Moses, as well as in the time of the dedication of Solomon's Temple. Further teachings in Jewish literature relate that, whether the visible glory hovered above the Temple, God's Presence was there. Scripture seems to bear witness to that fact.

According to Ezekiel Chapter 10, God took Ezekiel and clearly showed him the removal of God's Presence from Jerusalem. Surrounding Chapters of Ezekiel, as well as other contemporaries, give clues as to the sin condition within Jerusalem that made it impossible for God to dwell any longer amongst His people.

Among the long list of Judah's abominations were adherence to false prophets, robbery, murder, including assassinations of Judah's kings, as well as a refusal to remove idolatry from their lives. In short, the sins which prospered in Jerusalem, ones for which neither repentance nor atonement was made, effectively grieved God, Who then, removed His glory from that place. Shortly after the removal of that blessed presence, God's protective hand now withdrawn, Nebuchadnezzar burnt Solomon's Temple to the ground and destroyed the city, killing many, as well as taking captive many people.

GOD DWELLS ONLY WITH A HOLY PEOPLE

Here we can clearly see one of God's Ways. He desires to dwell in a Holy Place, with a Holy People. Sins, those unatoned under the First Covenant, stood as glaring abominations in the eyes of God.

Inhabitants of Judah, at that time, and for many centuries before, refused to live their life in accordance with conditions which God set in place, for His Presence in their midst. It would seem, by looking back at the First Covenant, God's patience and His Mercy were stretched to the farthest possible limits, before He finally removed His glory from that place.

WHO IS THE GLORY OF GOD?

Many Rabbis, in their writings online, hold to the concept that the Shekinah glory is really an outward display of the Holy Spirit. [43]Some Messianic believers feel the Shekinah glory was a manifestation of the Father's Presence in our midst. Christianity believes the Shekinah is actually a First Covenant manifestation of Yeshua. To this, it seems the book of Hebrews bears witness:

---

[43] Wikipedia online reference, cited in accordance with copyright rules.

Hebrews 1:3
"Who being the brightness of [his] glory, and the exact image of his person, and upholding all things by the word of his power, when he had by himself purged our sins, sat down on the right hand of the Majesty on high;"

Whether or not we are able to articulate exactly which member of the Godhead is the Glory of God, it is important to understand what it means to long for the Shekinah glory, as do many Christians. To hold a proper perspective, the longing should only be for the person of God, not for manifestation of His Presence! Let's look at one First Covenant example of the appearance of the Shekinah glory.

SOLOMON'S TEMPLE & SHEKINAH GLORY

If one did a study on the preparations of the Temple, there is clear evidence that, as all made ready in both the Temple and its attendants, they carefully followed a prescribe readiness, described by God within His Word[44]. This readiness assured that all participants met God's demands for holiness. Then, as the appointed day arrives, and the sanctified priests properly carry the Ark, they place it in the Temple's Holy of Holies, and then they removed the carrying

---

[44] The book, Foundations of Revival, (Biblical Evidence of Revival) by Jeanne Metcalf clearly explains the preparations of Solomon's Temple. To purchase a copy contact Cëgullah Publishing at cegullahpublishing.ca.

poles. After that, they exit and Solomon prays, after which the Shekinah glory falls:

2 Chronicles 7:1-4
"Now when Solomon had made an end of praying, the fire came down from heaven, and consumed the burnt offering and the sacrifices; and the glory of YeHoVaH filled the house. And the priests could not enter into the house of YeHoVaH, because the glory of YeHoVaH had filled YeHoVaH's house. And when all the children of Israel saw how the fire came down, and the glory of YeHoVaH upon the house, they bowed themselves with their faces to the ground upon the pavement, and worshipped, and praised YeHoVaH, saying, For he is good; for his mercy endures for ever. Then the king and all the people offered sacrifices before YeHoVaH."

This appearance of the Shekinah glory caused clear and definite reactions. First, the priests could not enter the house, due to the Presence of YeHoVaH. Second, the children of Israel fell prostrate on their faces and began to worship God, after which, they offered sacrifices to Him. It would seem from this scripture, as well as other scriptures, that the glory of God, upon arrival, definitely causes a great impact.

MOSES AND THE SHEKINAH GLORY
In Exodus 33, we have a record of Moses' conversation with God regarding both God's Presence and God's glory.

Exodus 33:1-3
"And YeHoVaH said unto Moses, Depart, [and] go up here, you and the people which you have brought up out of the land of Egypt, unto the land which I swore unto Abraham, to Isaac, and to Jacob, saying, Unto your seed will I give it: And I will send an angel before you; and I will drive out the Canaanite, the Amorite, and the Hittite, and the Perizzite, the Hivite, and the Jebusite: Unto a land flowing with milk and honey: for I will not go up in the midst of you; for you are a stiff-necked people: lest I consume you in the way."

God relayed to Moses His reason for not accompanying the children of Israel to the Promised Land. That reason was a decision of YeHoVaH to protect this disobedient, stiff-necked people from His Judgment, one in which would result in their death.

Exodus 33:4-6
"And when the people heard these evil tidings, they mourned: and no man did put on him his ornaments. For YeHoVaH had said unto Moses, Say unto the children of Israel, You [are] a stiff-necked people: I will come up into the midst of you in a moment, and consume you: therefore now put off your ornaments from you, that I may know what to do unto you. And the children of Israel stripped themselves of their ornaments by the mount Horeb."

Upon hearing the decree of God, the people obeyed YeHoVaH. Moses then set up the Tent of Meeting for any who wanted to repent and come before YeHoVaH:

Exodus 33:7-8
"And Moses took the tabernacle, and pitched it without the camp, afar off from the camp, and called it the Tabernacle of the congregation. And it came to pass, [that] everyone which sought YeHoVaH went out unto the tabernacle of the congregation, which [was] without the camp45. And it came to pass, when Moses went out unto the tabernacle, [that] all the people rose up, and stood every man [at] his tent door, and looked after Moses, until he was gone into the tabernacle."

As Moses entered the Tabernacle, the Shekinah glory of God described here as the cloudy pillar, descended and stood at the door of the Tabernacle. There, Moses talked with God. The people saw this awesome sight and rose up and worshipped.

Exodus 33:9-11
"And it came to pass, as Moses entered into the tabernacle, the cloudy pillar descended, and stood [at] the door of the tabernacle, and [YeHoVaH] talked with Moses. And all the people saw the cloudy pillar stand [at] the tabernacle door: and all the people rose up and worshipped, every man [in]

---

[45] Bold and italics not in original text

his tent door. And YeHoVaH spoke unto Moses face to face, as a man speaks unto his friend. And he turned again into the camp: but his servant Joshua, the son of Nun, a young man, departed not out of the tabernacle."

Moses continues talking with God:

Exodus 33:12-13
"And Moses said unto YeHoVaH, See, you say unto me, Bring up this people: and you have not let me know whom you will send with me. Yet you have said, I know you by name, and you have also found grace in my sight. Now therefore, I pray you, if I have found grace in your sight, show me now your way, that I may know you, that I may find grace in your sight: and consider that this nation [is] your people."

Moses asks God, *if on the condition he has found favour with God,* will God please show Him His Ways, because Moses wanted to know God. Certainly, this shows us the heart of Moses. He knew to serve God well, and lead a people designed by God to be a holy nation, Moses must understand God. He must know His Ways.

Then Moses went on to ask God to consider the nation of Israel, before Him:

Exodus 33:14-16
"And he said, My presence shall go [with you], and I will give you rest. And he said unto him, If your presence go not [with me], carry us not up from here. For wherein shall it be known here that I and your people have found grace in your sight? [is it] not in that you go with us? so shall we be separated, I and your people, from all the people that [are] upon the face of the earth."

Here we can see God's promise to go with this people, as well as a promise to give Moses rest. Moses makes it clear that if God's presence would not go, he didn't want to go forward. Moses knew that God's favour upon His people rested in His Presence accompanying them, wherever they went. He also knew that God's people, called to be a separated people, were thus to be a very different people from all other people upon the face of the earth.

Exodus 33:17
"And YeHoVaH said unto Moses, I will do this thing also that you have spoken: for you have found grace in my sight, and I know you by name."

In this encounter between Moses and God, Moses makes it clear that he longs for a relationship with God. That certainly pleased God. Then, Moses moves on to asks to see God's glory.

Exodus 33:19-23
"And he said, I will make all my goodness pass before you, and I will proclaim the name of YeHoVaH before you; and will be gracious to whom I will be gracious, and will show mercy on whom I will show mercy. And he said, You cannot see my face: for there shall no man see me, and live. And YeHoVaH said, Behold, [there is] a place by me, and You shall stand upon a rock: And it shall come to pass, while my glory passes by, that I will put you in a cleft of the rock, and will cover you with my hand while I pass by: And I will take away my hand, and you shall see my back parts: but my face shall not be seen."

There is no doubt from this passage that there is a definite, intimate link here with the person of God and His glory. To see God's glory was to see the person of God. God then dwelled with man, seen in the Tabernacle of Moses as well as the Temple of Solomon.

FIRST COVENANT REFERENCE
John the Apostle, as he writes his gospel regarding Yeshua, makes it very clear that God, in the person of Yeshua, dwelt (or tabernacled) in our midst:

John 1:14
"And the Word was made flesh, and dwelt among us, (and we beheld his glory, the glory as of the only begotten of the Father,) full of grace and truth."

Dwelt	Strong's Greek Word # 4637	σκηνόω
		skay-no'-o
It means to fix one's tabernacle, abide (or live) in a tabernacle (or tent), tabernacle, to dwell.		

Here is a very clear statement that Yeshua, God's glory, tabernacled in our midst. In reference to that tabernacle, the gospel of John records Yeshua's word to the Jews:

John 2:19-22
"Jesus answered and said unto them, Destroy this temple, and in three days I will raise it up. Then said the Jews, Forty and six years was this temple in building, and will you rear it up in three days? But he spoke of the temple of his body. When therefore he was risen from the dead, his disciples remembered that he had said this unto them; and they believed the scripture, and the word which Jesus had said."

Yeshua's physical body, while He dwelt upon the earth, was the true Temple of God. His death and resurrection made it possible for believers, individually and corporately, to become the spiritual temple of God[46] upon the earth, as the Holy Spirit takes up residence within them.

---

[46] Ephesians 2:19-22. We looked at that reference earlier, in another chapter.

1 Corinthians 6:19
"What? know you not that your body is the temple of the Holy Ghost which is in you, which you have of God, and you are not your own?"

Thus, as the Temple of God, the emphasis *of ownership* is not on the person, but rather on God's ownership. Such ownership requires special concessions to our behaviour, for which purpose YeHoVaH implanted His Holy Spirit and admonishes us to be filled with the Spirit.

Ephesians 5:18
"And be not drunk with wine, wherein is excess; but be filled with the Spirit;"

Furthermore, New Testament scriptures make it clear that believers must live differently than those who do not believe, just as Moses declared a separate behaviour for the children of Israel who camped before YeHoVaH. [47]

God desired them to live as a holy nation, separated unto Him alone, and He requires the same of born again believers:

---

[47] Exodus 33:14-16 as recorded on an earlier page

1 Peter 1:15-16
"But as he which has called you is holy, so be holy in all manner of conversation; Because it is written, Be holy; for I am holy."

God's character is one of total righteousness, and all His works are holy.

Psalm 145:17
"YeHoVaH is righteous in all his ways, and holy in all his works."

New Testament, born again believers are one of God's greatest works. We are a purchased possession, redeemed by the precious blood of the Lamb of God. God gave us His best, can we give Him any less? Certainly not! We lay before Him our lives, no longer living for our own wants and desires, but rather for those on His Heart, for His honour and glory.

How does all this relate to understanding God's ways, regarding His glory? First, we see that God desires to dwell with His People and has made great pains to make that possible. That fact thus shows an important call of God to all believers. It is a call to walk with the One who created the heavens and the earth and all that is in them. It is a privileged call to walk with the One who wants to walk with us. To make that walk successful, in both God's eyes and the believer's, we must walk it out with Him, His Way because His ways are best. While salvation opens the door to Eternal Life, that is the final goal. Day by day, after salvation's call, we get to experience God unfolding His Glorious person to us, so we can know Him intimately.

Therefore, our leaving this world, to be with Him eternally, is as simple as continuing on our walk with Him, a walk we are accustomed to, here upon the earth. It is good for believers to remember this fact that God designed us to be with Him eternally, but we are not to miss the call to walk with Him now.

As we walk with God, daily, we have our part to play for sure. Even though our sins are 100% atoned by Yeshua and there is no way that work will ever be removed, it is imperative that we chose to reflect God's Ways in our life. We do that by living a holy life. Again, this means we cannot live as we please, doing whatever we think is correct, like those who lived in Israel in the time of the book of Judges:

Judges 17:6
"In those days there was no king in Israel, but every man did that which was right in his own eyes."

If believers wish to really know God, to know His Ways, we begin by recognizing and then agreeing with His standard of holiness outlined in the Word of God.

Even though believers are positionally sanctified, having been set apart for God's Kingdom, the next step is to go in the direction for which we were separated:

Leviticus 20:7
"Sanctify yourselves therefore and be holy: for I am YeHoVaH your God."

1 Peter 1:15-16
"But as he which has called you is holy, so be holy in all manner of conversation; Because it is written, Be holy; for I am holy."

As you can see from the above two scriptures, the Apostle Peter quoted the First Covenant command to be holy, as God gave it to the Israelites. If we did not have any responsibility to walk in the direction of holiness, if that responsibility had changed at the cross, Peter would not see fit to quote the scripture.

One of God's Ways is to issue the call, and then leave the answer of that call to us. We are called in Messiah. That call is to be "holy", and it is our choice whether of not we answer it. That means we yield to the work of the Holy Spirit to make us living examples of the character of God. The more we know of God, the more we desire Him, and to look like Him. Isn't that a far better goal than to simply receive salvation to escape the fires of hell?

Pushing in with God to look like Yeshua, we align our hearts and lives to flow from that place of change, and thus, we will experience, more intensely, God's glory, just as did Moses. We will shine forth, then, with certain aspects of God's glory. Yeshua was the radiance of God's glory. Surely His children, dedicated to Him, in every aspect of their life, can show part of that glory to others

Hebrews 1:1-4
"God, who at different times and in various ways spoke in time past unto the fathers by the prophets, Has in these last days spoken unto us by his Son, whom he has appointed heir of all things, by whom also he made the worlds; Who being the brightness of his glory48, and the exact image of his person, and upholding all things by the word of his power, when he had by himself purged our sins, sat down on the right hand of the Majesty on high; Being made so much better than the angels, as he has by inheritance obtained a more excellent name than they."

Is God's glory, shining through the character of His people not a better goal for believers? Is this perhaps the reflection that God desires to see for His children? It could be argued, biblically, that is exactly what God desires, and hence, our focus on God's glory, to see it manifested in our lives should not be on experiencing

---
[48] Bold and italics not in original text

the cloud of His glory, but rather showing the radiance of it as we live out our lives before God, here on earth.

Of course, that does not mean that God's Shekinah glory will never again return to the earth as it did under the First Covenant. Ezekiel clearly prophesied a third temple,[49] which God's Shekinah glory inhabits, but for now, believers are God's Temple to show His glory.

CHAPTER'S SUMMARY:
As we look at gaining an understanding of God's Ways, we see that He desires to dwell with His People. In the New Testament, He has made it so very easy, as He purchased believers and cleansed them through the mercies of the Second Covenant in Yeshua's blood, after which, the Holy Spirit now comes and dwell within them. Certainly, this means that we cannot live as we please. We must, rather, align our lives with God's Word, living a life pleasing to Him, one that befits His Presence within our vessels.

Furthermore, as we looked at God's Presence, His Shekinah glory, we see that Presence convicted of sin, as seen in the passage we studied in Exodus 33. God's people repented and then God promised to go with them to the Promised Land, when earlier He said He

---

[49] *Ezekiel Chapter 40 and Revelation 21:2*

would not go for He would consume them due to their stiff-necked behaviour. As believers today, let us not be found with stiff-necked behaviour and in doing so, grieve YeHoVaH Who so wonderfully saved us!

Regarding God's Ways, in this chapter, we see His delight in His children, especially those who seek Him for Who He is, and for a true learning of His Ways. We also see that we, God's children, have a destiny to become like Yeshua and in doing so, give others around us a partial glimpse into God's Glory.

As we leave this chapter, let's remember several things about God's glory. Let us remember that the Shekinah glory is a wonderful display of God's glory, and it was seen in Yeshua. As long as we live our lives in accordance with God's plan, becoming like His Son, Yeshua, we too can refract God's Glory. Also, there is one more thing to remember. God's Presence, under the First Covenant and the New, as the Holy Spirit brings it forth, holds the very nature of God. Part of that nature is seen as Yeshua spoke of the Holy Spirit in the Second Covenant: He convicts of sin.[50] Let' us not get caught up in the eternal manifestations and miss the internal change God desires for believers.

---

[50] *John 16:8-10*

Let's remember:

God's Presence, in any state, manifested or seen in the Shekinah glory, is a convicting power[51], for He longs to see His people to be holy, as He is Holy.

---

[51] Please note that God's Presence keeps His people awake, alive and in the Spirit, not slumbering and living in sin.

CONCLUSION

"So God created man in his own image[52], in the image of God created he him; male and female created he them."
Genesis 1:27

SIN ENTERED THE world, and through its influence, marred that image of God, nevertheless, God still desires to see His image in each human being that walks upon the face of this earth. To these ends, God gave the law and sent the prophets, culminating in the gift of His Son, Yeshua. Those in Yeshua, by faith, have God's Spirit, dwelling within them, to bring forth the image of God.

---

[52] Walking through this book together, we have seen that God desires His people to resemble the image He placed in them at creation.

To attain those ends, as we walk with YeHoVaH daily through our lives, we must learn to look at our ways, aligning them with what God requires, understanding what God commands His children:

Mark 12:29-31[53]
"And Jesus answered him, The first of all the commandments is, Hear, O Israel; YeHoVaH our God is one Lord: And you shall love YeHoVaH your God with all your heart, and with all your soul, and with all your mind, and with all your strength: this is the first commandment. And the second is like, namely this, You shall love your neighbour as your self. There is none other commandment greater than these."

As we consider our ways, with the idea of aligning them with God's desire for us, we see that we must also undertake to learn the ways of YeHoVaH for they are very different than that which we see in other human beings. Understanding our God, as well as what He requires of us, will help to make us better believers, and help to establish what God so longs to see upon this earth: His people resembling the Son of God, Yeshua, in their actions towards God and towards

---

[53] We have looked at this often before, thus, stressing the importance of the message in passages like this one.

man. This image, indeed, is what God longs to see in His people: *A reflection of His Son!*

Let us join our hearts together and aim towards allowing God to do a work in us, to satisfy the longing of His Heart!

Let us be willing servants, ready to draw near to God, listen to His heart and allow His Hand to mold us into the image in which He created us!

APPENDIX

YeHoVaH[54]

A Name to Honour

If, today, someone asked you to tell them the name of your earthly father, without hesitation you would declare it. If, for some reason, you did not know the identity of your earthly father, you would say so. You might even give an explanation as to why that might be so. Thus said, if asked to relate the name of your heavenly Father, today, would you do so with ease, or would you draw a blank?

Most of Christendom, today, is totally ignorant as to the name of the Father, as well as the way to pronounce it. As the author of this book, I would like to join the ranks of those who wish to relate that name to the world. When we stand before the Father on the day, we give an account for our deeds in this body, it would be a good thing to know Him, His Name.

---

[54] Based on information given by Michael Rood. Some from his work entitled, The Chronological Bible, and some from his YouTube videos. For more information see page 28 of the Chronological Bible.

Did you know that the name of the Father appears at least 6,828 times in the Hebrew scriptures? Scribes recorded it with four specific Hebrew letters. They are as follows:

י	Pronounced yode, or yod
ה	Pronounced as hey
ו	Pronounced as Vav
ה	Pronounced as hey

For centuries, whenever the Jews come across these 4 letters they simply say, Adonai, or Ha Shem (meaning the name). They refuse to pronounce the name for several reasons, some of which we will look at momentarily. For now, let us look at whether their tradition affected Christianity. That we can easily do by looking at our Bibles to see the 4-letter name of the Father either written or substituted.

A quick look reveals that our KVJ Bibles, as well as many other versions, the 4-letter name presented to readers is a 4-letter English word, "LORD" [55]. Whether intentional or not, Christendom has followed the ancient tradition of the Jews.

<u>An Ancient Tradition</u>
In early second century times [56] Rabbis hid the pronunciation of the holy name of God. They did this by omitting the vowel pointings, which are necessary

---

[55] In some translations it is GOD.
[56] Some scholars even dating further back.

to make the name pronounceable. Hence, as they carefully wrote the scriptures, their omittance of the vowel pointings made the name unpronounceable. Historians believe there were two reasons why they did this:

According to Josephus, Rome, under the rule of Domitian, 81 to 96 CE, put to death anyone using the name of the Jewish or Christian God.
Many believe that the Rabbis borrowed a tradition from pagans, whereby the name of their god was considered too holy to mention, so they called him "Baal" meaning Lord. The Jews adopted this practice and most still practice it today, even some Messianic Jews!

Tradition Continues
Bible translators followed their tradition for many reasons which are not presently known. It is possible, they forgot the pronunciation of the name, but more than likely, those who knew it, hid it.[57]. Whatever the reason, following this tradition caused Christians to continue in this tradition.

Does that tradition offend the Heavenly Father?

If indeed its origin was Baal worship, then we can give a resounding Amen to the fact it offends God. In addition, as we look at scripture, we see the Almighty

---

[57] According to some, the Jews secretly knew the name.

was not pleased with this, for His Heart desires all to enjoy salvation, including the Gentiles. How can that happen if they do not know upon what name they should call? Scripture [58] clearly says in the end times, Gentiles will know His name and call upon it to receive salvation. Obviously, for that to happen, they must know the name of YeHoVaH (יְהֹוָה).

An Historic Discovery

Today, some Hebrew scholars [59] have searched the world over for Hebrew manuscripts. In doing so, they have found many Hebrew documents have the full name with vowels and therefore the pronunciation of the name. These scholars may different slightly in pronunciation, but nevertheless, they are making the name of YeHoVaH known today.

OUR SAVIOUR'S NAME HIDDEN

In looking at the Hebrew root of the name of the Father, pronounced *Yah-Ho **Vah'***, and looking at another scripture, we see something amazing about our Saviour. In speaking of the Prophet, the one the Father would send and to whom all must listen and

---

[58] Jeremiah 16:1-21
[59] Nehemiah Gordon, a Hebrew scholar, according to his testimony, found the name of the Father with all vowel pointings in the Aleppo Codex, and through his efforts and those of others discovered that name with vowels pointings in over 2000 manuscripts.

obey, YeHoVaH said that His name would be in the name of the Prophet.

Exodus 23:21 "Beware of him, and obey his voice, provoke him not; for he will not pardon your transgressions[60]: *for my name [is] in him."*

Our Saviour's name, as given by the angel was "Yehoshua", which means Salvation.

That name, with its Hebrew letters reads as:

י	**Pronounced yode or yod**
ה	**Pronounced hey**
ו	**Pronounced vav**
שׁ	Pronounced shin
ע	Pronounced ayin

The name of the Father (יְהֹוָה) is in the name of the Son! The first three letters of YeHoVaH show it! (Yod, Heh, Vav). Is it so amazing that the name of our Father is in the true name of the One YeHoVaH sent to redeem us!

Honour the Father's Name

Throughout this book, and all later books, as well as all accompanying audios and PowerPoints, it is the author's intention to widely use, proclaim and

---

[60] Please keep in mind that Yeshua bore the punishment for your sins. Your sins were not pardoned, they were atoned!

continually pronounce the name of the Father, as well as the name of Yeshua. Indeed, this breaks with tradition of many, however, thus far as we have shared the news of the Father's name and use Yeshua's birth name, reception has been excellent.

Name Challenge
Since, as of this reading, you are no longer ignorant of your heavenly Father's name, we invite you to join the unofficial network of proclaimers of the Father's name and shout it to the house tops. In doing so, you honour the Heavenly Father, our Savour Yeshua, and the Holy Spirit.

ABOUT THE KING JAMES VERSION

Scriptures quoted in this book *originate* from the KJV **public domain version** of the Bible, which means, no copyright exists on this version of the scripture. While some find this translation outdated, Jeanne, trained in the KJV still finds this version helpful, and uses it in all her books.

In using KJV, however, it is good to remember the following:
- Some words in the KJV have changed meaning over the centuries. To understand such words, look up the root word in its original language. In doing so, the meaning stands out. For example. KJV uses the word "conversation" however, in its original language it means moral character, or behaviour.
- When KJV spoke of humanity as a whole, they said, "man". When you read that word, or hear another person speak in reference to the scriptures and the term, "man", know it refers to all humankind, not a specific gender.
- Due to tradition, the name of the Father, YeHoVaH appears as LORD, or at times as Jehovah. However, in all Jeanne's manuscripts, YeHoVaH's name replaces the term LORD. To learn more read "A Name to Honour", located in the Appendix section.

SALVATION'S MESSAGE
Yeshua, when walking on earth, said this:
> John 3:14-18
>> *14 And as Moses lifted up the serpent in the wilderness, even so must the Son of man be lifted up: 15 That whosoever believes in him should not perish but have eternal life. 16 For God so loved the world, that he gave his only begotten Son, that whosoever believes in him should not perish, but have everlasting life. 17 For God sent not his Son into the world to condemn the world; but that the world through him might be saved. 18 He that believes on him is not condemned: but he that believes not is condemned already, because he hath not believed in the name of the only begotten Son of God.*

During the time of Moses, the children of Israel, in the wilderness, rebelled against God, at which time poisonous serpents infiltrated the camp, killing many of the people. After seeking YeHoVaH for a solution to the problem, Moses followed God's instructions and made a bronze serpent fashioned and erected it on a pole in sight of the people. Whosoever wanted to live, must acknowledge their rebellion against YeHoVaH, and in doing so, look upon the erected pole and bronze serpent, to YeHoVaH, who gave them life in place of death, then they would live.

Yeshua said, just as Moses erected that bronze serpent in the wilderness, He would be lifted up. This referred to the event, in the future, of Yeshua's crucifixion. During the time when the serpent hung on that pole, whosoever wanted to live and not die from the serpent's bite must acknowledge their rebellion, their sin against YeHoVaH.

Likewise, for those who wish to live eternally, they must look upon the cross of the crucified One, to YeHoVaH, who provided life for them. This was an act of love for all humankind, necessary because man is born from Adam, and thus is born with an inherent sin.

Secondly, man sins. The consequence of sin is death, and eternal death, wherein man will spend an eternity in darkness, away from YeHoVaH. Unfortunately, there is nothing humanly possible to reverse those consequences. Even if a person had made a genuine decision never to sin again, and for some reason they succeeded, all their good deeds and good living would not erase the penalty of eternal death.

There is only ***one way*** for Eternal Life to touch a person's life. That is the way Yeshua explained to His listeners:
through the cross.

Salvation comes by understanding these facts:
- Yeshua, being the Son of God and the fulfilment of the scriptures, never sinned.
- YeHoVaH, on behalf of every human being on the earth, chose to make Yeshua become as sin, in His Eyes, so that Yeshua might pay the penalty for sin, for all of humanity.
- Yeshua paid that penalty. He died on the cross and was buried in a tomb.
- Three days later, He rose again, appearing to His disciples, to show them the reality of His resurrection, to show them God vindicated Him and made Him both Lord and Messiah.
- Yeshua could not stay in the tomb, because "death" comes to all who sin, but since Yeshua never sinned, therefore, death could not hold Him in the grave.
- All those who come to Yeshua, to receive Him as their Saviour, receive liberty from sin and from its horrible consequence, eternal death.
- Additionally, they enter YeHoVaH's Kingdom and receive eternal life, as well as another gift: **The Righteousness of Messiah.**
- After salvation, when YeHoVaH looks upon a believer in Messiah, He sees Yeshua's perfect life and sees a redeemed believer, set aside for YeHoVaH.
- Since salvation has taken place in the believer, the Holy Spirit dwells within them.

- All it takes to receive salvation from YeHoVaH is receiving His Messiah, fully repenting from sinning against God. [61] YeHoVaH even gives the believer the faith to receive His gift of Salvation!

The Apostle Paul put it this way:
Ephesians 2:8
"For by grace are ye saved through faith; and that not of yourselves: it is the gift of God"

When you pray the following prayer, realize we present it here to get you started in your walk with YeHoVaH. Living out your salvation depends upon your commitment to follow through *from this point, onward*. From the moment of your commitment and onward, dear one, please seek YeHoVaH for His help in all things, including help to make your life align with truth, and in the end be a praise unto His name, forever!

---

[61] And against man. When a person steals, etc. they sin against both God and man. PLEASE NOTE: all references to "man", either by scripture or the author, refers to all humankind, not a specific gender.

SINNER'S PRAYER & LIFETIME COMMITMENT

Heavenly, Father:
I acknowledge before You, Lord, that I am a sinner. I understand sin's punishment is a life without You, for all eternity. Thank You for sending Yeshua to the earth, as the Messiah. I understand now that He died in my place, to take my punishment for my sins. I believe You raised Yeshua from the dead, and now that I've I accepted Him as my personal Saviour, my old life dies, and my new life begins.

I humbly ask You, Lord, to forgive me of my sins, and as of this moment, I receive Yeshua as my Mashiach. I open my heart to receive the works of the cross that You provided for me through Yeshua, and with Your help, I will walk away from my sin, turning my back upon my own will and ways. I will now live my life seeking to obey Your Word and Your will. Help me to live, from this point onward, in a manner pleasing to You.

*****

One more thing:

Remember, this gospel message comes with power. When you hear it, the Kingdom of God draws near to you. When you repent of your sins and receive Salvation, the Kingdom of God moves within. You cannot see it, feel it, or tell it from an outward observance. It is accepted, received, and lived out by faith! Seek out other believers in Messiah and may

God bless you richly as you live your live, now, completely for Him!

So now, be sure and tell someone!
Remember that a person believes with the heart unto righteousness and confesses with their mouth unto salvation, as spoken about in *Romans 10:10:*

> *10 For with the heart man believes unto righteousness; and with the mouth confession is made unto salvation*

BASICS OF
THE ANCIENT HEBREW PICTURE LANGUAGE[62]

Whenever you translate something from one language to another, there is always a risk of compromising the depth of the original language, especially if that language is not as expressive as the original, and does not hold words, which precisely articulate the meaning. Such is the case when translating from Hebrew to English. For example, to translate a Hebrew 'tallit', which is an important part of the traditional Jewish garment, worn by men, we have no such English word to express it.

The word tallit means, "little tent", but the translators simply interpreted it as tent. In our language, however, when we think of a tent, we know there are large tents and pup tents. However, 'tallit', if properly interpreted, is, in reality, a woven shawl traditionally made on a white background, in which people wrap themselves when they are in prayer alone with God. Today we call that a "prayer shawl". Translating the word, 'tallit' as 'tent', hardly means the same thing.

This is but one instance where early interpretations of scripture erred, and because of that one little mistake, many believers think that Acts 18:3, that described the Apostle Paul as abiding with 'tentmakers', means that

---

[62] For those who teach our courses, we have helps available such as PowerPoints. Contact us for more details.

Paul made tents, meaning outdoor shelters, when in fact, as a trained Pharisee, Paul made 'prayer shawls'. This is but one instance but there are many other places in the Word, where translators overlooked cultural expressions and the like, and thus, gave the reader a different meaning than the original transcripts.

We must always ensure, when looking at Hebrew words with our English mind, that we consider these things and remember that Hebraic thinking differs greatly from our Western world. Differences in thinking, between Hebraic and Western thought, would take a lot of time to explain, so for now, keep in mind, that the Hebraic language is 'relational' while the Western World is not. The Hebrew picture language explains that point well.

AN AGRICULTURAL LANGUAGE
The early Hebrew language, like other languages, began as an agriculturally based language explaining ideas of their civilization with 'pictures' relative to their environment. The alphabet, in this early language, was comprised of letters, whose design indicated certain parts of the body to describe certain words. Other letters used well-known animals, such as the ox and others, to describe common things during their civilization's existence. For example, the letter "aleph", the first letter, pictured an ox's head, and the second letter "bet" represented a tent where the family lived. To explain this in further detail, we will look at

the word, "Father", which uses both the "aleph" and the "bet".

THE HEBREW WORD FOR FATHER

Hebrew words usually have a base of three characters. The first two characters are known as Parent Root, the characters following are known as the Child Root. [63]
The word for Father is Ab. In both English and Hebrew, it consists of two major letters. In English, the letters are A and B. In the Hebrew, they are ALEPH and BET.

In English, we read this way

⟶

from Left to Right,
In Hebrew, we read this way

◀┄┄┄┄┄┄

from Right to Left.

For us, this seems rather awkward, but nevertheless, keep that in mind as you read the letters below.

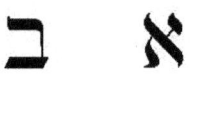

BET   ALEPH

---

[63] When understanding "Parent and Child Root" it is only in the most simplistic format that it is easy to interpret. Past four or five characters, it is more difficult to grasp.

In the picture language, an Ox's head represents the Aleph and the Bet is pictured as a dwelling place, or a tent. The ox is a strong animal, used to pull carts and carry heavy burdens and the like. Within a tent, the family lived. Putting this together, you have a picture of a strong person over the house, capable of carrying burdens. Hence, the Hebrew picture language describes the Father as this: *The strong person over the house equipped to carry burdens.* Since the picture shows the strong one over the house, the father gives account to God for all that happens within jurisdiction.

This picture, quite profound in its imagery, also projects the scripture principle that God hold's the father responsible for the family. He, the strongest one created to carry burdens, God holds into accountability for what goes on in his household. Also, as you look at the Hebrew pictograph language, keep in mind it is relational, rather than abstract, as in the English language. A study of it produces amazing thoughts from which we can learn much. As long as we keep our findings within the Biblical framework and we ensure our interpretation [64] aligns with the original context of the scripture in its natural setting, our findings should be accurate[65].

---

[64] The meaning of *Hebrew words* explained in the book by use of the Hebraic picture language, came as the author sought God for an understanding of that word.

[65] For more information, investigate the many sources who speak of the Hebrew Picture language. Some you might research are

SCRIPTURE INDEX

1

1 Chronicles 16:27 173
1 Corinthians 1: 27 129
1 Corinthians 15:31....... 17
1 Corinthians 6:19 212
1 John 4:18 171
1 Kings 19:13 119
1 Kings 19:14 119
1 Kings 19:18 120
1 Peter 1:15-16 ...... 213, 215
1 Peter 1:3-5 54
1 Peter 2:24 146
1 Peter 4:15-19 111
1 Samuel 17: 45-47 131
1 Samuel 25:2-3 148
1 Samuel 25:37-38 150
1 Timothy 1:18-20 106

2

2 Chronicles 16:9 134
2 Chronicles 7:1-4 205
2 Corinthians 10: 3 104
2 Peter 1:1-4 97
2 Peter 1:4 107
2 Peter 1:5-12 102
2 Samuel 12:14 50
2 Timothy 3:1-7 20

A

Acts 13:22 133
Acts 17:6 28
Acts 5:41 111
Acts 7:2 127

C

Colossians 1:12-14 100

D

Daniel 11:32 b 250
Daniel 2:20-23 174
Deuteronomy 18:1-2 53
Deuteronomy 30:16 63
Deuteronomy 32: 4 68
Deuteronomy 32:7-9 53
Deuteronomy 34:10 151
Deuteronomy 4:2 69
Deuteronomy 4:20 52
Deuteronomy 6:5 .... 18, 63
Deuteronomy 9:13-14 45

E

Ephesians 1:3 55
Ephesians 2:19-20 .....77, 82

---

ancient-hebrew.org, or Hebrew4Christians, or look at works by Frank Seekins.

Ephesians 2:19-22 211
Ephesians 2:21-22 78
Ephesians 2:8 236
Ephesians 5:18 212
Exodus 19: 5-6 47
Exodus 20:15 65
Exodus 23:21 230
Exodus 24:16 .... 200, 201
Exodus 33:12-13 208
Exodus 33:1-3 206
Exodus 33:14 212
Exodus 33:14-16 ... 197, 209
Exodus 33:17 209
Exodus 33:19-23 210
Exodus 33:4-6 206
Exodus 33:7-8 207
Exodus 33:9-11 207
Exodus 34:6 67
Exodus 40:35 200
Ezekiel 36:21-23 50
Ezekiel 48:35 173

G

Galatians 2:20 17
Galatians 4:6-7 160
Galatians 5:16-17 105
Galatians 5:4-9 89
Genesis 1:27 221
Genesis 18: 18 128
Genesis 22:14 172

H

Habakkuk 1:1-4 32
Habakkuk 2:1 .... 31, 33
Habakkuk 2:4-7 33
Hebrews 1:1-4 216
Hebrews 1:3 .... 88, 204
Hebrews 10:38 133
Hebrews 11:17-40 190
Hebrews 11:24-27 151
Hebrews 11:8-12 128
Hebrews 12:1-3 188
Hebrews 4:12-13 94
Hebrews 7:25 27
Hebrews 9:1-10 80
Hosea 13:14 175

I

Isaiah 28:16 84
Isaiah 29:13 .... 92, 95
Isaiah 44:22 48
Isaiah 52:5 50
Isaiah 53:1-12 143
Isaiah 53:1-9 185
Isaiah 55:9 156

J

James 1:23-25 14
Jeremiah 16:1-2 229
Jeremiah 24:7 48
Jeremiah 29:11 193
Jeremiah 4:1 48
Job 1:1 180

Job 1:9-12 181
Job 13:13-15 179
John 1:14 210
John 12: 24-26 108
John 14:27 172
John 16:33 183
John 16:8-10 218
John 2:19-22 211
John 5:39 .... 85, 175
John 5:46 85
Joshua 24:2 126
Judges 17:6 214

L

Leviticus 20:7 215
Luke 10:27 18
Luke 21:1-6 152
Luke 24:44-48 86
Luke 24:44-49 79
Luke 4:18-19 173

M

Malachi 3:7 48
Mark 12:29-31 222
Matthew 15:8-9 ... 21, 92, 95
Matthew 16:11-12 91
Matthew 21:42-44 84
Matthew 22:37-40 64
Matthew 26:36-39 184
Matthew 4:4 173

P

Proverbs 30:5-6 69
Psalm 100:5 68
Psalm 103:1-5 171
Psalm 103:7 43
Psalm 105:16-22............183
Psalm 108: 4.....................68
Psalm 118:22 84
Psalm 119: 160................70
Psalm 119:105 70
Psalm 119:11 70
Psalm 119:128 70
Psalm 119:138 69
Psalm 119:140 70
Psalm 119:142 68
Psalm 119:151 69
Psalm 119:54 70
Psalm 119:89 ....59, 60
Psalm 119:98 70
Psalm 136:1-26 164
Psalm 139:7 198
Psalm 139:8-12 199
Psalm 145:17 213
Psalm 147:1-5 172
Psalm 19:1 167
Psalm 19:2-4 a...............167
Psalm 25:10 69
Psalm 31: 19-24.............141
Psalm 31:11-13 140
Psalm 31:14-18 140
Psalm 31:19-20 139
Psalm 32:7 174

Psalm 33:4 68
Psalm 43:3 68
Psalm 57:10 68
Psalm 68:1-4 174
Psalm 73:16-20 35
Psalm 73:20-26 36
Psalm 89: 14 71
Psalm 89:1-4 .... 159, 161

R

Revelation 2: 12-17 90
Romans 10:10: 238
Romans 11: 25-36 123
Romans 11:11-12 121
Romans 11:19-26 122
Romans 11:33-36 .. 117, 124
Romans 2:24 51
Romans 8:13-14 104
Romans 8:15 161
Romans 8:28 .... 164, 177
Romans 8:35-39 194

T

Titus 2:1-15 72

Z

Zephaniah 3: 17-18 109
Zephaniah 3:17-18 97

Books By Jeanne Metcalf

An Arsenal of Powerful Prayers -
Volume 1: Scriptural Prayers to Move Mountains
978-1-926489-24-7

An Arsenal of Powerful Prayers -
Volume 2: Scriptural Prayers to Shatter Strongholds
978-1-926489-97-1

Above Artificial Intelligence
Finding God in a World of A.I.
978-1-926489-93-3

Arising Incense
A Believer's Priesthood
978-1-926489-57-5

An End Time Church in Transition
Preparing for the King's Return
978-1-926489-98-8

Bible Study Basics
A Closer Look at God's Word
978-1-998561-02-5

Candidate for A Miracle
Wisdom from the Miracles of Yeshua
978-1-926489-88-9

Deceived
How Errors in a Faith System Affect Both God & His People
978-1-998561-04-9

Foundations of Revival
Biblical Evidence for Revival
978-1-926489-52-0

His Reflection
What God longs to see in His People
978-1-926489-15-5

Heaven's Greater Government
Behind the Scenes of Earth's Events
978-1-926489-44-5

In The Name of Yehovah We Set Up Our Banners
Biblical Use of Banners
978-1-926489-33-9

It's All About Heaven
As Pictured in Scripture
978-1-926489-32-2

Kingdom Keys for Kingdom Kids
Walking in Kingdom Power
978-1-926489-91-9

Molded for the Miraculous
Why God made You
978-1-926489-89-6

Our Secure Faith Heritage
Foundational Truths to an Unshakeable Walk with God
978-1-998561-00-1

Releasing the Impossible
The Limitless Power of Intercession
Volume 1: Intercessions from the Author's Life
978-1-926489-45-2

Releasing the Impossible
The Limitless Power of Intercession
Volume 2: Intercessions from Biblical Characters
Workbook: Both Volumes compiled in Workbook.
978-1-926489-46-9

Salvation Depicted in a Meal [66]
An Hebraic Christian Guide to Passover
978-0-9813194-0-7

---

[66] Haggadah (Guide) for a Christian Passover. No Workbook.

The Coming Deception
How to Recognize the Man of Sin, the Son of Perdition
978-1-998561-06-3

The Jeremiah Generation
God's Response to Injustice
978-1-926489-36-0

The Warrior Bride-
God's Kingdom Advancing Through Spiritual Warfare
978-1-926489-42-1

Thy Kingdom Come
Entering God's Rest in Prayer
978-1-926489-83-4

Watching, Waiting, Warning
Obeying Yeshua's Command to Watch & Pray
978-1-926489-80-3

When Nations Rumble
A Study of the Book of Amos
978-1-926489-25-4

Worship in Spirit and In Truth
The Tabernacle of David - Past, Present & Future
978-1-926489-38-4

About Jeanne Metcalf

Jeanne believes the Word of God opens a door to help every believer to know their God. That knowledge, once gleaned and retained, makes strong believers to help them stand in the real world in which we live, no matter their vocation.

With these convictions in mind, Jeanne, inspired and led by the Holy Spirit, began to write in the 1990's. Soon she developed inductive 67 style Bible Studies and self-published them for her students to use. With her major goal to equip the saints, she found that her sound teachings, presented with clarity and simplicity, made an impact. As long as her listeners put in their valuable time to study scripture and took Jeanne's advice to call upon the Holy Spirit to help them, they became powerful believers, transformed, prepared and ready to stand in their generation.

Today, past students who studied the Bible with Jeanne, as well current new students, testify as to the validity of Jeanne's writing and teaching gift. They love the clarity and simplicity of the Word as she presents it in a refreshing straightforward format. Thus, they encouraged Jeanne to make her books more widely available.

Therefore, Jeanne began Cegullah Publishing, and then a year later, opened Cegullah Apologetic Academy. The

---

[67] In the inductive Bible Study method, believers learn first by reading and studying the Word on their own, then they glean from the textbook. This study method often gives a better foundation to a believer's faith than sitting through lectures or speaker related teachings.

academy, in addition to presenting accredited, Bible Study material, invites all believers to read or study the Word of God, and thereby, be strong in YeHoVaH and the strength of His might.

A greater availability of Jeanne's works (as well as other authors which Cegullah Publishing looks forward to publishing in the future), opens doors for more people to know their God and do exploits!

> **"But the people that know their God**
> **shall be strong and do exploits".**
> **Daniel 11:32 b**

P.S. Recent inquiries require acknowledging the correct way to formally address Jeanne. While she is comfortable with people addressing her on a first name basis, her official title is Rev. Dr. Jeanne Metcalf.

As a Christian entity, we present apologetics and publish books on that subject.

OUR PUBLISHING ARM provides opportunities for our reading audience to explore pertinent topics which steady, reaffirm, and help them to walk out their life in victory.

OUR ACADEMY ARM presents accredited courses for those students who wish to study to obtain their degree, either bachelor, master, or doctorate.

Contact Information
www.cegullahpublishing.ca
Publishing Arm: *cegullahpublishing@gmail.com*
Academy Arm: *apologeticsacademy@outlook.com*

www.ingramcontent.com/pod-product-compliance
Lightning Source LLC
Chambersburg PA
CBHW062157080426
42734CB00010B/1731